T5-AFL-761

Criminal Justice
Recent Scholarship

Edited by
Marilyn McShane and Frank P. Williams III

A Series from LFB Scholarly

Racial Prejudice, Juror Empathy, and Sentencing in Death Penalty Cases

Bryan C. Edelman

LFB Scholarly Publishing LLC
New York 2006

Library of Congress Cataloging-in-Publication Data

Edelman, Bryan C., 1974-
Racial prejudice, juror empathy, and sentencing in death penalty cases / Bryan C. Edelman.
p. cm. -- (Criminal justice : recent scholarship)
Includes bibliographical references and index.
ISBN 1-59332-127-9 (alk. paper)
1. Verdict--United States. 2. Jury--United States. 3. Capital punishment--United States. 4. Discrimination in criminal justice administration--United States. 5. Race discrimination--United States. I. Title. II. Series: Criminal justice (LFB Scholarly Publishing LLC)
KF9685.E33 2006
345.73'0773--dc22

2005031122

ISBN 1-59332-127-9

Printed on acid-free 250-year-life paper.

Manufactured in the United States of America.

TABLE OF CONTENTS

INTRODUCTION..1

CHAPTER 1
DEATH PENALTY JURISPRUDENCE AND
SENTENCING SYSTEMS IN AMERICA..7

CHAPTER 2
RACE DISPARITIES WITHIN THE POST-FURMAN
SYSTEM: ARCHIVAL LITERATURE..21

CHAPTER 3
THE POST-TRIAL INTERVIEW RESEARCH ON
RACE AND SENTENCING...39

CHAPTER 4
THE EXPERIMENTAL RESEARCH ON RACE
AND SENTENCING...47

CHAPTER 5
DEVELOPING A MODEL OF JUROR AND JURY
DECISION-MAKING..59

CHAPTER 6
RESEARCH DESIGN AND
PROCEDURES..79

CHAPTER 7
RESULTS OF ANALYSIS AND MODELS......117

CHAPTER 8
DISCUSSION OF JUROR DECISION-MAKING: WHAT DOES IT ALL MEAN......145

APPENDIX A......157

APPENDIX B......159

APPENDIX C......181

APPENDIX D......187

REFERENCES......199

SUBJECT INDEX......207

ACKNOWLEDGEMENTS

Over the years I have had the support and guidance of my mentors, friends, and family. Ronald Dillehay kept me focused and always offered his support, time, and expertise when needed. Without him, this work would not have been completed. I would also like to thank Edward Bronson, Markus Kemmelmeier, David Coulson, and Bill Evans, for their contributions to this research. Finally, I would like to thank William Bowers and the Capital Jury Project for supplying me with the data and assistance which made this project possible.

INTRODUCTION

The traditional American system of beliefs that encouraged overt forms of racism and segregation has been replaced by an egalitarian value system, which developed out of the civil rights movement. Unlike its predecessor, this normative system of beliefs admonishes against discriminatory behavior and encourages equal treatment across racial groups. As a result of this change, open expressions of racism (e.g., lynching) have been significantly reduced. Yet, the civil rights movement did not extinguish prejudice; rather, it forced it to metamorphize into a more subtle form that operates beneath the surface. Public opinion on segregation is just one example of how this new breed of discrimination functions. On the surface, the public tends to support interracially mixed neighborhoods. However, this support begins to waver when respondents' neighborhoods are threatened by an influx of minorities (Gaertner & Dovidio, 1986). This subtle form of racism is more difficult to identify, and as a result, more arduous to combat.

At first glance, the steps taken to address race within the criminal justice system appear to comport with the egalitarian value structure, and the standards of equality set forth by the Warren Court in the fifties and sixties. For example, efforts have been made to expand minorities' participation in the judicial process by attempting to broaden the representativeness of the jury pool. Yet, when one delves deeper into contemporary judicial decisions pertinent to race and the application of justice, it becomes apparent that these decisions are quite insidious in that they merely add to a growing body of jurisprudence that focuses attention on the core values or *symbolic legality* of criminal procedure, rather than on the biased outcomes these procedures produce (Haney, 1991). As a result, a system that allows for and perpetuates racial discrimination has been developed and defended on the pretext that in its most abstract form, these procedure are "race neutral."

The preference to dismiss final outcomes and blindly hold fast to the notion that the procedure is fundamentally sound is no more evident than when one examines the development of jurisprudence within the context of capital punishment. The field and experimental research on race and sentencing clearly illustrates that these procedures produce racial disparities. Archival studies have documented a pattern of race-of-victim discrimination throughout the capital trial process (see GAO, 1990). The experimental literature suggests that the race of the defendant has an effect on how participants evaluate evidence and reach sentencing conclusions (see Mazzella & Feingold, 1994). These findings are buttressed in the post-trial juror interview literature, which has shown both race-of-defendant and race-of-victim effects (see Bowers, Steiner, & Sandys, 2001). The Supreme Court has chosen to dismiss this mounting body of evidence and has placed its faith in the notion that the written procedures that have been put into law guide jurors' discretion in a fashion that is consistent with the values set forth in the Constitution. Yet, a closer look at the complex structure of the contemporary sentencing systems that have developed out of capital punishment statutes, and the guidance these procedures provide raises questions as to the source of the Court's faith.

Jurors bring their pre-existing schemas and attitudes toward the defendant and victim into the sentencing phase of a capital trial. These attitudes are developed from the stereotypes jurors hold, the evidence presented during the guilt phase of the trial, the ensuing deliberations, and often from the pretrial publicity that capital crimes tend to produce. After convicting a defendant for a capital offense, jurors are asked to make a subjective causal judgment and decide upon the proper punishment on the basis of that judgment. At this stage of the process, contradictory evidence is proffered that points to negative internal causes (e.g., prior history of violence), and to external or mitigating internal causes (e.g., extreme poverty and youth). Additional information is provided about the value of the victim's life and the impact that the crime has had on his or her friends and family. After all of this evidence has been presented, jurors are given convoluted instructions on how and when to evaluate this amalgam of subjective material to reach a sentencing decision, and are then sent to deliberate. The sentencing phase of a capital trial can aptly be described as novel, subjective, emotional, and complex. Contrary to the Supreme Court's opinion, the sentencing schemes that have been developed in an effort to reduce discriminatory sentencing may create the type of setting where subtle forms of racism are most likely to occur.

This study develops and tests a model that attempts to explain how and when non-legal factors such as race are most likely to affect juries' and jurors' sentencing decisions. The initial model's focus is on a victim evaluation and defendant attribution process.

According to the victim evaluation component, the murder of a positively evaluated victim is perceived to be more severe than the murder of a less positively evaluated victim. The impact of race on this evaluation is contingent upon jurors' tendencies to categorize the victim as an in-group or out-group member on the premise of race. Under certain conditions, jurors will perceive themselves to be similar to the victim on self-relevant attributes when the victim is categorized as an in-group member. Perceived similarity should cultivate positive affect and empathy, which should have a positive influence on victim evaluations. In addition, perceived dissimilarity should lead to the withholding of positive affect and empathy, which will have a negative influence on victim evaluations.

According to the defendant attribution component, a negative internal attribution tends to support a death sentence. An external and some internal attributions support a life sentence. A negative internal attribution is likely to ensue when jurors' defendant schemas are associated with a race-based stereotype, and the murder conviction is consistent with that stereotype. As a result, evidence will be either refuted or accepted and integrated into jurors' defendant schemas on the basis of whether it is perceived to support or conflict with the attribution hypothesis.

Whether or not the effects of race on pre-deliberation sentence positions will carry over and influence the jury's final sentence outcome is predicted to be moderated by the clarity of the normative structure that governs the sentencing task and the salience of jurors' egalitarian values. Evidence ambiguity, jury composition, instruction comprehension, and instruction guidance were predicted to have an impact on the development of the normative structure in a capital trial, the perceived presence or absence of non-racial justifications for discriminatory sentencing, and the likelihood that white jurors will activate their egalitarian values. These factors come into play once deliberations begin.

The Capital Jury Project (CJP) provided secondary data from face-to-face interviews conducted with over 1,100 capital jurors from 14 states. The final sample encompassed 76 black-defendant/white-victim cases, 63 black-defendant/black-victim cases, and 367 jurors. Additional case specific data were collected from Lexis/Nexis published opinions. These data, coupled with juror case descriptions, were used to create a "deathworthiness" scale, so that cases could be classified together on the basis of crime, defendant, and victim(s) characteristics. This served as a control for the factual differences among cases.

The original model received mixed support. Although not all of the predictions were confirmed, several extralegal factors, including race, were found to have an influence on how evidence was evaluated and ultimately how decisions were made. The subtle race-of-victim effect that has been reported in much of the archival literature did appear to influence sentencing. White jurors were found to empathize more with white than black victims and evaluate them more positively. In addition, killers of white victims had a more difficult time convincing white jurors to take mitigating factors into account than killers of blacks. However, the race-of-defendant effects that have been documented in the experimental literature were not uncovered within the current study.

Taking these results and the literature on empathy into account, a new model was developed that included empathy toward the defendant and defendant evaluations.

Although empathy toward the defendant was found to affect defendant evaluations, victim empathy had a far grater influence on the decision-making process. Empathy toward the victim had a direct negative influence on white jurors' defendant evaluations and also had an indirect effect on how mitigating evidence was used.

Once again, the race-of-victim was found to have a subtle influence on jurors' sentencing positions. White jurors were more likely to discount mitigating evidence that would justify a life sentence when the victim was white. The race of the victim also had an indirect effect on the evaluation of the defendant that was mediated through empathy toward the victim. Jurors empathized more with the victim when she was a member of the in-group than when she was a member of the out-group. As a result, killers of whites were evaluated less positively than killers of blacks. These two indirect effects suggest that white jurors were less likely to hold a life sentence position when a black defendant was convicted for murdering a white victim.

These findings have several important implications pertaining to a defendant's constitutional rights to a trial free of racial bias and prejudice. Decisions which have expanded the role of non-statutory aggravating evidence may exacerbate the effects of race. Because defendant and mitigating evidence evaluations are affected by empathy toward the victim and ensuing victim evaluations, evidence that cultivates this type of empathy will ultimately limit the importance of the defendant's life circumstances on juror's sentencing decisions. In conflict with the Supreme Court's assurances, this study suggests that it may not be the worst of the worst who are being sentenced to death, bur rather the killers of the best of the best.

CHAPTER 1

DEATH PENALTY JURISPRUDENCE AND SENTENCING SYSTEMS IN AMERICA

EARLY HISTORY AND CONSTITUTIONAL CHALLENGES

Capital punishment in America can be traced back to the arrival of the European settlers. The first recorded execution took place in the Jamestown Colony of Virginia in 1608. Attempts to tinker with the system of death also have an early history, dating back to Thomas Jefferson's efforts in the Virginia legislature to limit capital punishment to crimes of murder and treason. States began passing laws against mandatory death sentences in 1838 and by 1963 all mandatory capital punishment laws had been revised to discretionary death penalty statutes (Bohm, 1999).

Challenges to the constitutional legality of discretionary capital systems were first raised in 1968, when the Supreme Court heard two cases dealing with the discretion granted to the jury and the prosecutor.[1] In *U.S. v. Jackson* (390 U.S. 570 [1968]), the Court declared that the provision of the federal kidnapping statute—which required that the death penalty only be imposed upon the recommendation of the jury—encouraged defendants to avoid a death sentence by waiving their right to a jury trial, violating their Sixth Amendments' due process rights. In *Witherspoon v. Illinois* 391 U.S. 510 [1968]), the Court held that the prosecutor must show that a juror's attitude towards the death penalty would prevent him or her from making an impartial decision about punishment, before that person can be excluded from sitting on a death penalty jury.

By the early 1970s, the abolitionist movement began to raise Fourteenth Amendment[2] challenges to jury discretion and to the racial disparities that discretionary sentencing systems tended to produce. Both defendants in *Crampton v. Ohio* (398 U.S. 936 [1970]) and *McGautha v. California* (402 U.S. 183 [1971]) argued that the jury's unfettered sentencing discretion resulted in arbitrary and capricious outcomes in violation of the Due Process Clause. Race came to the forefront in *Maxwell v. Bishop* (398 U.S. 262), and in *Spenkeling v. Wainwright* (440 U.S. 976 [1979]), where the petitioners brought claims of discriminatory sentencing in violation of the Equal Protection Clause. In the former, the appellant submitted data hinting at discrimination against black offenders. In the latter, data were submitted indicating that murderers of whites were more likely to be sentenced to death than murderers of blacks. The Court rejected each of these Fourteenth Amendment challenges and upheld jury discretion.

In 1972, the abolitionist movement made an important tactical move and shifted its strategy from a Fourteenth to an Eighth Amendment argument. Unlike the Fourteenth, the Eighth Amendment does not require the showing of purposeful discrimination.[3] In *Furman v. Georgia* (408 U.S. 238 [1972]), the court ruled in a five-to-four

---

[1] This represents a review of events pertinent to this study. Thus, it does not encapsulate the entire body of jurisprudence on capital punishment.

[2] The Fourteenth Amendment reads, "…nor shall any State deprive any person of life, liberty, or property, without due process of law; nor deny to any person within its jurisdiction the equal protection of the laws."

[3] The Eighth Amendment reads, "Excessive bail shall not be required, nor excessive fines imposed, nor cruel and unusual punishments inflicted."

decision in favor of the petitioner, invalidating 629 death sentences in forty states (Death Penalty Information Center, n.d.).

Furman raised the same argument brought by *McGautha*, but claimed that the "unguided" jury discretion prescribed to juries in Georgia's statute could result in arbitrary and capricious sentencing, in violation of the Eighth Amendment's prohibition against "cruel and unusual punishment." The Court did not rule that the death penalty was inherently "cruel and unusual punishment," only that the current procedure by which it was administered was unconstitutional. This left the door open for procedural reform. Within months states changed existing legislation to appease the concerns raised in *Furman*.

Post-Furman Sentencing Statutes: Guided Discretion

Two basic approaches were devised: the *North Carolina model* and the *Georgia model*. North Carolina addressed the reservations raised in *Furman* by eliminating jury discretion altogether, calling for mandatory death sentences for certain crimes defined by statute. The Georgia model addressed the Court's concerns by devising a system of "guided discretion."

This system bifurcates a capital trial into two proceedings, a guilt phase and a sentencing phase. A defendant must be charged and found guilty of a capital crime as defined by statute before the trial can enter into the sentencing phase. The Georgia model also limits jury discretion by restricting the types of homicides that are eligible for death to homicides having the presence of certain circumstances or *aggravating factors*.[4] "Aggravating factors make a murder more reprehensible than other homicides and thus support the death penalty" (Latzer, 1998, p. 45). Some examples of statutory aggravators include: (1) the offense of murder, rape, armed robbery, or kidnapping was committed by a person with a prior record of conviction for a capital

---

[4] Two recent Supreme Court decisions have reduced the scope of death eligible crimes. In *Roper v. Simmons* (No. 03-0633 [2005]) the Court ruled that it is a violation of the Eighth Amendment to execute juveniles; thus, invalidating 72 death sentences. In *Atkins v. Virginia,* (No. 01-8452 [2002]), a six-to-three majority ruled that executing mentally retarded criminals is also a violation of the Eighth Amendment.

felony; (2) the offender committed the offense of murder for himself or another, for the purpose of receiving money or any other thing of monetary value; (3) the offender caused or directed another to commit murder or committed murder as an agent or employee of another person; (4) the person intentionally commits the murder in the course of committing or attempting to commit kidnapping, burglary, robbery, aggravated sexual assault, arson, or obstruction or retaliation; and (5) the person murders an individual under six years of age.

During the sentencing phase, a jury must vote unanimously that the state has proven beyond a reasonable doubt that at least one of the aggravating circumstances defined in the Georgia statute is present before a defendant can be declared "death eligible."

Jurors are also presented with evidence in support of *mitigating factors*. "Mitigating factors are circumstances of the crime or characteristics of the defendant that make the offense less reprehensible and therefore support a less harsh punishment" (Latzer, 1998, p. 45). Some examples of mitigating circumstances include: (1) whether or not defendant acted under extreme duress or under the substantial domination of another person; (2) whether or not at the time of the offense the capacity of the defendant to appreciate the criminality of his conduct or to conform his conduct to the requirements of law was impaired as a result of mental disease or defect, or the affects of intoxication; (3) the age of the defendant at the time of the crime; (4) whether or not the offense was committed under circumstances which the defendant reasonably believed to be a moral justification or extenuation for his or her conduct; any (5) any other circumstance which extenuates the gravity of the crime even though it is not a legal excuse for the crime.

The Georgia model puts no limitations on the types of evidence that a defendant can present in support of mitigation. While a jury must vote unanimously beyond a reasonable doubt that a statutory aggravating factor exists, mitigating factors require a lower standard of proof and do not require unanimity. Each juror can choose to encompass mitigating factors in her decision if she so chooses.

Both models faced Eighth Amendment challenges in 1976. Mandatory sentencing was struck down in *Woodson v. North Carolina* (428 U.S. 280). "Guided discretion" passed judicial scrutiny in a seven-to-two decision in *Gregg v. Georgia* (428 U.S. 153). In *Gregg*, the Court ruled that death penalty laws that provide specific guidelines for the jury to follow when deciding on death are acceptable (Hans & Vidmar, 1986). The Court concluded that, "While some jury discretion still exists the discretion to be exercised is controlled by clear and objective standards so as to produce non-discriminatory application." Since *Gregg*, 36 states have revised their statutes under the rubric of guided discretion.

CLASSIFYING SENTENCING SCHEMES

Guided discretion systems vary by task (i.e., weighing vs. non-weighing) instruction specificity, and by final decision-maker. By disregarding these differences, researchers may be overlooking some of the features of the sentencing task phenomenon that lead to race-based sentencing, oversimplifying the sentencing task, and incorrectly generalizing their results to capital punishment schemes that differ significantly from the one under analysis. The varying levels of complexity and jury discretion that these systems allow may moderate the effects of race on sentencing. Thus, the magnitude of the race effect may be exacerbated within schemes that are likely to lead to heuristic decision-making, and minimized within those that constrain jurors, by providing sufficient guidance on how to evaluate evidence and reach a decision. As a result, it is important to take these differences into account.

The weighing system requires each juror to compare the cumulative weight of mitigating evidence to that of the aggravating evidence and determine which direction the theoretical scale tips. If the mitigating evidence outweighs the aggravating evidence, then the sentence is life. If the scale tips towards the aggravating evidence, then death is an option. Of the 36 states that have capital punishment statutes on the books, 13 are classified *as non-weighing states*.[5] The remaining 23 are classified as *weighing states*.[6] The scheme by which

---

[5] Arizona, Georgia, Illinois, Kentucky, Louisiana, Montana, New Mexico, South Carolina, Virginia, Washington, Texas, Oregon & Wyoming

[6] Alabama, Arkansas, California, Colorado, Connecticut, Delaware, Florida, Idaho, Indiana, Maryland, Mississippi, Missouri, Nebraska, Nevada, New

weighing process operates varies from state-to-state. Some statutes offer no guidance to jurors on how to weigh factors (e.g., Florida). Other states do; however, the specificity of these standards varies. For example, the Utah Statute (§ 76-3-207) reads as follows (emphasis added):

> (b) The death penalty shall only be imposed if, after considering the totality of the aggravating and mitigating circumstances, the jury is *persuaded beyond a reasonable doubt that total aggravation outweighs total mitigation, and is further persuaded, beyond a reasonable doubt*, that the imposition of the *death penalty is justified* and appropriate in the circumstances. If the jury reports *unanimous agreement* to impose the sentence of death, the court shall discharge the jury and shall impose the sentence of death.
>
> (c) If the jury is *unable* to reach a *unanimous decision* imposing the sentence of death or the state is not seeking the death penalty, the *jury shall then determine whether the penalty of life in prison without parole shall be imposed*, except as provided in Subsection 76-3-207.5(2). The penalty of life in prison without parole shall *only be imposed if the jury determines that the sentence of life in prison without parole is appropriate*. If the jury reports agreement by *ten jurors or more* to impose the sentence of *life in prison without parole*, the court shall discharge the jury and shall impose the sentence of life in prison without parole. If ten jurors or more do not agree upon a sentence of life in prison without parole, the court shall discharge the jury and impose an indeterminate prison term of not less than 20 years and which may be for life.

Other weighing statutes are less specific. California (§ 190.3), for example, does not define the standard of proof in the determination of

---

Hampshire, New Jersey, North Carolina, Ohio, Oklahoma, Pennsylvania, South Dakota, Utah & Tennessee whether the aggravating evidence outweighs the mitigating evidence. In some *non-weighing states*, jurors are not given guidance on how to use aggravating and mitigating evidence to reach a sentencing decision. Other non-weighing states can be classified as *special issues* states. Under this system, jurors are posed with several questions. In Texas for example they must answer two questions (Tex. Code Crim. Proc. art. §37.071 (2002)):[7]

(1) Whether there is a probability that the defendant would commit criminal acts of violence that would constitute a continuing threat to society;
(2) Whether the defendant actually caused the death of the deceased or did not actually cause the death of the deceased but intended to kill the deceased or another or anticipated that a human life would be taken.

In Oregon, the jury must answer the following four questions (ORS §163.105 (1)(b)):

(1) Whether the conduct of the defendant that caused the death of the deceased was committed deliberately and with the reasonable expectation that death of the deceased or another would result;
(2) Whether there is a probability that the defendant would commit criminal acts of violence that would constitute a continuing threat to society;
(3) If raised by the evidence, whether the conduct of the defendant in killing the deceased was unreasonable in response to the provocation, if any, by the deceased;
(4) Whether the defendant should receive a death sentence.

[7] The Texas statute and its application have come under fire in recent Supreme Court decisions. In *Smith V. Texas* (No. 04-5323 [2004]), for exaple, the Court agreed that the failure to instruct jurors that proper consideration be given to all mitigating evidence was error.

Death penalty statutes can be further classified into jury or judge sentencing systems. In the former, the jury is charged with determining the sentence. A sentence of death must be a unanimous decision and is binding on the trial judge. Twenty-seven of the thirty-six states with death penalty statutes on the books fall within the jury-sentencing scheme. The remaining nine are classified into one of three judge-sentencing schemes: (1) the judge has sole sentencing discretion; (2) a three-judge panel decides upon the sentence; or (3) the judge makes a sentencing decision after the jury recommends a sentence. Systems in the third category do not require juries to vote unanimously on their sentencing recommendation. Delaware, Indiana, Florida, and Alabama fall within this category. The constitutionality of judge-sentencing schemes was brought into question in *Ring v. Arizona* (122 S. Ct. 2428 [2002]). This decision immediately invalidated death sentences in Arizona, Idaho, Colorado and Nebraska, where sentencing is completely taken out of the hands of the jury. Although the ramifications of this ruling within jury recommendation states are unclear, in *Schriro v. Summerlin* (No. 03 526 [2004]) the Supreme Court ruled that *Ring* would not apply retroactively.

POST-GREGG JURISPRUDENCE AFFECTING "GUIDED DISCRETION"

Jurisprudence concerning the discretion granted to jurors and prosecutors has developed considerably since *Gregg*. Much of this development has concentrated on the use of non-statutory evidence, the constitutionality of such evidence, and its role in the decision-making process. Non-statutory evidence consists of evidence that addresses a factor that is not defined within a state's death penalty statute. The use of non-statutory mitigating evidence came to the forefront in *Lockett v. Ohio* (438 U.S. 586 [1978]). In *Lockett*, the Court ruled that the Ohio death penalty statute violated the Constitution because it narrowed the range of character and offense evidence a defendant could present as mitigation:

> ...the Ohio statute, in limiting the range of mitigating circumstances which may be considered by the sentencer, was constitutionally infirm, since the Eighth and Fourteenth

> Amendments required that the sentencer, in all but the rarest kind of capital case, must not be precluded from considering, as a mitigating factor, any aspect of a defendant's character or record and any of the circumstances of the offense that the defendant proffered as a basis for a sentence less than death...

Three Supreme Court decisions in 1983 addressed the use of non-statutory aggravating evidence. In *Zant v. Stephens* (462 U.S. 862 [1983]), the Supreme Court ruled that:

> The U.S. Constitution does not require a sentencing jury in a capital case to ignore other possible aggravating factors in the process of sentencing, from among the class of persons eligible for the death penalty, those defendants who will actually be sentenced to death.

In *California v. Ramos* (463 U.S. 992 [1983]), the U.S. Supreme Court ruled that:

> Once the jury finds that the defendant falls within the legislatively defined category of persons eligible for the death penalty, as did respondent's jury in determining the truth of the alleged special circumstance, the jury then is free to consider a myriad of factors to determine whether death is the appropriate punishment.

Finally, in *Barclay v. Florida* (463 U.S. 939 [1983]), the Court ruled that:

> We have never suggested that the United States Constitution requires that the sentencing process should be transformed into a rigid and mechanical parsing of statutory aggravating factors. But to attempt to separate the sentencer's decision from his experiences would inevitably do precisely that. It is entirely fitting for the moral, factual, and legal judgment of judges and juries to play a meaningful role in sentencing. We expect that sentencers will exercise their discretion in their own way and to the best of their ability.

Taken together, these three decisions have moved the pendulum back towards "unguided discretion" and have added complexity to a decision-making task which has been found to be convoluted and difficult for jurors and research participants alike to understand (see Luginbuhl & Howe, 1995; Diamond, 1993; Lynch & Haney, 2000; Weiner, Prichard, & Weston, 1995). The Court has effectively lowered the constitutional burden placed on capital punishment states. In essence, "guided discretion" can be limited to the question of "death eligibility." Once the "death eligible" threshold has been met, it is permissible to allow the jury to use a myriad of factors unrelated to the statutory defined aggravators to reach a final sentencing decision with the caveat that the non-statutory evidence cannot be used until after the defendant has been declared "death eligible."

This non-statutory material can be emotionally charged and highly prejudicial toward the defendant, yet it is presented in conjunction with the statutory aggravating evidence during the sentencing phase of the trial. It can only be assumed that the Court is confident that jurors can and do disregard this evidence when deciding upon death eligibility. However, there are often no guidelines to help jurors identify what is to be used and what is to be set-aside in this process. As a result, jurors are likely to draw on evidence that has been ostensibly presented by the state for the sentencing decision to determine death eligibility. For example, statute 921.141(7) of the Florida criminal code allows victim impact statements to be admitted into evidence, but not for the purpose of deciding upon "death eligibility."

> Once the prosecution has provided evidence of the existence of one or more aggravating circumstances as described in subsection (5), the prosecution may introduce, and subsequently argue, victim impact evidence...to demonstrate the victim's uniqueness as an individual human being...

This type of evidence may be incorrectly used by a juror or jury to establish the presence of a given aggravator, particularly when the factor is ambiguous. Factor (h), "The capital felony was especially heinous, atrocious, or cruel," provides a good example. Emotional expressions of loss may enhance the perceived cruelty of the crime, and as a result prove the existence of the aggravator. This concern was recently rejected by the Supreme Court in *Bell v. Cone* (NO. 04-394 [2005]). In *Bell*, the Court ruled that the terms "especially heinous, atrocious or cruel" do not fail to guide a jury on how to apply the aggravating factor.

Decisions since 1983 have continued to reduce the burden placed on the state by broadening the types of evidence that fall under the nomenclature of non-statutory evidence. In *Payne v. Tennessee* (1991) (501 U.S. 808), the Court violated the principle of stare decisis[8] and overturned its decisions in *Booth v. Maryland* (482 U.S. 496 [1987]) and *South Carolina v. Gathers* (490 U.S. 805 [1989]). *Booth* had precluded the admission of victim impact statements in capital trials on the grounds that such evidence poses an unacceptable risk that sentences could be handed down in an arbitrary manner, since the focus of such statements is on the victim, a factor unrelated to the blameworthiness of the defendant. In *Booth*, the Court ruled that the

> Defendant often will not know the victim, and therefore will have no knowledge about the existence or characteristics of the victim's family...Allowing the jury to rely on a victim impact statement therefore could result in imposing the death sentence because of factors about which the defendant was unaware, and that were irrelevant to the decision to kill. This evidence thus could divert the jury's attention away from the defendant's background and record, and the circumstances of the crime.

In *Payne*, the Court ruled that victim impact evidence is simply another method of informing the sentencing authority about the specific harm caused by the crime. The decision went on to say:

---

[8] Policy of courts to stand by precedent and not disturb settled points.

Booth was decided by a 5 to 4 margin with Powell, Brennan, Marshall, Blackmun, and Stevens in the majority and White, Rehnquist, O'Connor, and Scalia in the minority. *Payne* came up after Marshall and Brennan were not longer on the Court. The two new Justices, Kennedy and Souter shifted the balance of the Court towards inclusion. *Payne* was decided by a 6 to 3 majority with Rehnquist, White, O'Connor, Scalia, Kennedy, and Souter in the majority and Marshall, Blackmun, and Stevens in the minority.

> Booth's holding unfairly weighted the scales in a capital trial, inasmuch as, while virtually no limits were placed on the relevant mitigating evidence a capital defendant might introduce concerning his own circumstances, the state was barred from either offering a glimpse of the life which a defendant chose to extinguish or demonstrating the loss to the victim's family and to society which resulted from the defendant's homicide.

This shift towards "unguided discretion", unbridled admissibility, and enhanced decision-task complexity increases the role that illegitimate factors (e.g., race, emotion, etc.) are likely to play in sentencing decisions. This opens the door to the arbitrary and capricious sentencing admonished against by the *Furman* Court. Evidence such as victim impact statements can shift jurors' focus away from the defendant and towards the victim(s). In an emotionally charged environment such as that of a capital trial, when race (e.g., black-defendant/white-victim homicide) is salient and the decision-making task unclear, there is a danger that jurors will resort to the type of victim evaluation process that was the bedrock underlying the *Booth* decision and an afterthought in *Payne*. Writing the majority opinion in *Payne*, Rehnquist wrote:

> Payne echoes the concern voiced in *Booth*'s case that the admission of victim impact evidence permits a jury to find that defendants whose victims were assets to their community are more deserving of punishment than those whose victims are perceived to be less worthy…victim impact evidence is not offered to encourage comparative judgments of this kind—for instance, that the killer of a hardworking, devoted parent deserves the death penalty, but that the murderer of a reprobate does not.

If jurors engage in this type of comparative decision-making process, then sentences will not be guided by statute, but by jurors' evaluations of the victim's life. When these evaluations are affected by unconstitutional factors (e.g., race, SES), then the life of a white, affluent male may be perceived to be more valuable than that of a poor, unemployed African American by a jury dominated by a white majority.

In the spirit of *symbolic legality*, the *Payne* decision went on to provide an avenue for redress for these types of arguments. "In the event that evidence is introduced that is so unduly prejudicial that it renders the trial fundamentally unfair, the Due Process Clause of the Fourteenth Amendment provides a mechanism for relief." For all practical purposes, the Fourteenth Amendment as a remedy for race-based discrimination in the capital system was effectively eliminated in *McCleskey v. Kemp* (482 U.S. 920 [1987]).

In *McCleskey,* the appellant raised a Fourteenth Amendment equal protection challenge and submitted data—which came to be known as the Baldus Study—into evidence detailing broad racial sentencing disparities in the Georgia system. The Court accepted the validity of the findings, but rejected the claim that the statistical evidence alone provided sufficient proof to support McCleskey's claim. This reflects the Supreme Court's aversion to evidence that indicates that the Georgia Model of guided discretion has failed to redress the arbitrariness that was singled out in *Furman.*

The Court went on to set the standard for equal protection challenges, using those established in *Washington v. Davis* (426 U.S. 229 [1976]). This criterion requires appellants to provide evidence of intentional and purposeful discrimination in their capital trial, a difficult if not almost impossible burden to meet. To this date, the Court has rejected all Fourteenth Amendment equal protection challenges to the death penalty.

The Supreme Court has developed a substantial body of jurisprudence on the subject of capital punishment in the thirty years since *Furman.* As the *McCleskey* decision indicates, the Court's focus has centered on sentencing procedures, largely ignoring the disparate outcomes such sentencing schemes produce. As a result, state legislatures have developed complex sentencing structures that meet the demands set forth by the Court and concurrently create the illusion of a race neutral system that comports with society's egalitarian value system. These systems are likely to create situations in which the task is complex, information processing demands are high, and jurors' instruction comprehension is low. These are the types of contexts where race effects are most likely to surface.

CHAPTER 2

RACE DISPARITIES WITHIN THE POST-FURMAN SYSTEM: ARCHIVAL LITERATURE

There have been over forty archival studies since *Furman*, documenting the effects of illegitimate factors—including race—on sentencing decisions in the capital punishment system. These studies have varied in methodological complexity and with respect to the decision point(s) examined. Taken as a whole this body of research has shown a consistent trend within the post-*Furman* system: *Murderers of white victims suffer a higher probability of being sentenced to death than murderers of blacks.* This finding has been shown to be consistent across locations, time periods, and methodologies (see the GAO 1990 Report below). The race-of-victim effects appear to be strongest in the cases where the evidence is ambiguous in that it does not clearly support a life or death sentence. The archival research has not shown a strong race-of-defendant effect. Two conclusions can be drawn from this finding. It is possible that the race of the defendant does not have an impact on sentencing in the post-*Furman* system. It is also possible that the race of the defendant plays a role in sentencing, but the archival method is not able to detect its effects.

This chapter organizes the archival studies into two sections on the basis of their inclusion or exclusion of a "deathworthiness" or culpability scale within their design. These scales are used to classify cases on the basis of the severity of the crime, so that race effects can be properly evaluated. In order to show a pattern of racial bias, one must show that the system arbitrarily imposes death sentences in some cases within a class of cases with similar circumstances, which usually result in prison sentences. Under these circumstances, defendants sentenced to death cannot be distinguished in a legitimate way from defendants sentenced to life (Baldus, Woodworth, & Pulaski, 1990, p.14).

ARCHIVAL LITERATURE: FINDINGS

Studies Failing to Control for Case Evidence or "Deathworthiness"

The Anti-Drug Abuse Act of 1988 requires the government to study capital sentencing procedures to determine if race influences the likelihood that defendants will be sentenced to death. The General Accounting Office met this requirement in 1990.

The GAO included twenty-eight studies in its analysis and concluded that there is a pattern of race-of-victim effects in the charging, sentencing, and imposition phases of the post- *Furman* system that cannot be explained by aggravating circumstances or other legally relevant factors (e.g., prior record, culpability level, heinousness of the crime, and number of victims). Race effects were strongest at the earlier decision points of the process, where the relative magnitude of the effect size was most pronounced.

The effect of defendant race on sentencing was less clear. Although over half the studies found that the race of defendant influenced the likelihood of being charged with a capital crime or receiving the death penalty, the relationship varied across studies. Over three-fourths of the latter studies found that black defendants were more likely to receive the death penalty. The remaining found that white defendants were more likely to be sentenced to death. In some cases the race-of-defendant variable interacted with another factor, e.g., rural vs. urban area, or victim race. In other instances, it did not.

A recent update to the GAO report by Sorensen, Wallace, and Pilgrim (2001), looked at the archival studies on race and the death penalty conducted in the nineties. Fifteen studies from eleven death penalty states were included. The legal case variables found to be most consistently related to charging and/or sentencing were the presence of multiple victims, contemporaneous felonies, torture or mutilation, rape or a sexual motive, and prior history/record of violence.

Fourteen studies found evidence of a race-of-victim effect and eleven found evidence of a race-of-defendant effect. Seven studies focused on jury discretion. Of these, two showed a race-of-defendant effect; one supported a race-of-victim effect; and one a victim/offender interaction. Although nearly half of the studies on jury discretion did not find statistically significant evidence of racial bias, the patterns of racial disparities were similar to those found in earlier stages of the process. In addition, small sample sizes at this stage of the analysis may explain the non-significant results in these studies. The race-of-defendant effects were similar to those found in the GAO report. It was not clear whether it had an independent effect on sentencing or operated in conjunction with the race-of-victim variable.

Bowers and Pierce (1980) looked at the effects of race on sentencing in Florida, Georgia, Texas, and Ohio in the first five years after *Furman*. Data were collected from Supplementary Homicide Reports on felony circumstances of the crime; race of the victim and offender; the statutory, aggravating, and mitigating circumstances found by sentencing authorities; and the current status of the case in the appellate review process.

The researchers looked at several different decision points: charges at arraignment, first-degree murder indictments, first-degree murder convictions, and sentence decisions. The probability of a black-defendant/white-victim murder moving on to the next stage in Florida was higher than the probability of a black-defendant/black-victim murder at every stage of the process. The probability of a black/white murder resulting in a death sentence given a conviction was 47 percent in comparison to a black/black murder, which was 20 percent (Bowers & Pierce, 1980, p. 609). It is possible that black victim murders are qualitatively different from white victim homicides in that the former are less severe than the latter. Bowers and Pierce (1980) attempted to address this issue by examining a sub-sample that included murder cases with an accompanying felony crime (e.g., rape). Racial disparities continued to persist. The probability of a black/white murder resulting in a death sentence given a conviction for these cases was 51 percent in comparison to a black/black murder, which was 32 percent (Bowers & Pierce, 1980, p. 611).

Keil and Vito (1995) looked at race-of-victim effects on prosecutorial discretion and jury sentencing in Kentucky from 1976 to 1991. The researchers controlled for: concurrent felony (murder committed in conjunction with robbery, burglary, arson, rape or sodomy), number of victims, silence (accused killed the victim to prevent testimony), violent history, multiple aggravating circumstances, and victim/offender relationship (stranger or otherwise). The sub-sample for the sentencing analysis consisted of 158 defendants. Results indicated that blacks who killed whites were more likely to be sentenced to death than any other defendant/victim racial combination (Keil & Vito, 1995, p. 27).

Williams and Holcomb (2004) examined the effects of the victim's gender and race on sentence outcomes in Ohio. Data were collected on homicides that occurred between 1981 and 1994 from Supplemental Homicide Reports, the Office of the Ohio Public Defender, the Office of the Ohio Attorney General, and the Ohio Department of Rehabilitation and Correction. The researchers controlled for the offender's gender and age, the location of the murder, whether or not the victim was under 12 years of age, accompanying felonies, the number of victims, and the use of a gun. Due to limitations in the data, the effects of the independent variables on earlier decision-making points were not explored.

Results from a logistic regression found that homicides with white victims were more likely to result in a death sentence than those with black victims. A victim race-gender interaction effect was also found. Specifically, killers of white female victims were more likely to be sentenced to death than killers of other than white females. No race-of-offender effects were found to be significant.

Murphy's (1984) study on race and sentencing included all death eligible murder indictments handed down in Cook County, Illinois from 1977 to 1980. Data were collected from police reports, witness memoranda in the clerk's files, and the Public Defender's Office. Murphy (1984) looked at several different decision points: conviction, motion for death hearing, death eligible decision, and sentence.

Neither the race of the defendant nor the victim was found to be related to conviction. However, victim race was significantly related to sentencing. After controlling for felony murder, Murphy found that black defendants who were convicted of killing white victims were more likely than black defendants convicted of killing black victims to be sentenced to death, 15 percent vs. 6 percent respectively. In addition, black defendants convicted of killing white victims during the commission of an armed robbery were about twice as likely to be sentenced to death than black defendants convicted of killing black victims, 11 percent vs. 5 percent respectively. The race of the offender was not found to be a significant predictor of sentence outcomes. It is important to note that only 18 death sentences were included in this study and only felony circumstance was controlled for. In addition, although Murphy looked at several different decisions points, she excluded the pretrial decision points, i.e., prosecutor decision to file capital charges.

Although these studies document race effects in a multitude of states with varying sentencing schemes, it cannot be ruled out that white victim homicides are simply more aggravated than black victim homicides. The following section reviews studies that have attempted to rule out this possibility by developing various measures designed to classify cases as similar to one another on the basis of the severity of the crime.

Controlling for “Deathworthiness”

The ideal study would be to examine cases with identical fact patterns where only the race of the victim and defendant were free to vary. If it were discovered that similar cases resulted in different outcomes within categories, then it would be reasonable to assume that illegitimate factors were having an effect. However, cases with similar fact patterns are a rarity. As a result, researchers have developed *a priori* and empirical methods to classify cases with different facts into categories as a function of their "deathworthiness" or level of "culpability." The *a priori* approach classifies cases on the basis of criteria that should predict appropriate sentencing. Empirical approaches classify cases by legitimate case characteristics that have been shown statistically to explain the observed sentencing results (Baldus et al., 1990, p. 47).

Few of the studies within the archival literature incorporate culpability scales into their designs. Of these, even fewer look at the effects of race on jury discretion. The studies, which have looked at jury discretion, tend to show a race-of-victim effect. This effect appears to be strongest in the midrange culpability level cases. Researchers have labeled this finding the "liberation hypothesis." This term, which first appeared in *The American Jury*, was developed to explain disagreements between juries and judges. Kalvin and Zeisel postulated that "disagreement arises because doubts about the evidence free the jury to follow sentiment" (Kalvin & Zeisel, 1966, p. 166).

The "liberation hypothesis" has since been applied to discrepancies in capital sentencing. According to this application, trial evidence overwhelmingly in favor of a life or death sentence usually concludes with an outcome consistent with the evidence. However, when the evidence is ambiguous in that it favors neither the prosecution nor the defense, the likelihood that illegitimate factors such as race, gender, and attractiveness will have an effect on sentencing increases. This finding may be explained by the theory of aversive racism. According to the theory, white Americans are unlikely to discriminate when the normative structure within a given situation is clear and egalitarian norms are salient (Gaertner & Dovidio, 1986). Evidence strength may be a factor that impinges upon the normative structure within the sentencing task. White jurors may find it difficult to justify their sentencing positions on the basis of non-racial terms when the evidence overwhelmingly supports a contradictory outcome. Support for the "liberation hypothesis" is described herein.

Arnold Barnett (1985) developed an *a priori* three-dimensional empirical system to classify cases using narrative summaries of over 600 homicide cases. The dimensions include: (1) the certainty the defendant is a deliberate killer; (2) the status of the victim; and (3) the heinousness of the killing.

The first dimension reflects the degree of certainty that the accused was the killer and whether the defendant acted intentionally to cause the victim's death. The case is given a zero (reflects a relatively weak case in terms of certainty and/or deliberateness); one (if neither a zero nor a two is justified); or two (exceptionally strong evidence that the killing was not an isolated, aberrant act of passion or panic).

The second dimension concerns the relationship between the victim and the accused: was the victim a stranger; was the victim killed in his or her official capacity; or did the defendant know the victim?

The case is scored a zero or a one, with the latter indicating a higher chance of a death sentence.

The final dimension is based on whether or not the defendant killed in self-defense and whether or not the murder was vile (i.e., multiple victims, psychological torture or sexual abuse, and those involving bizarre weapons or mutilated bodies). Cases are rated zero (a killing in self-defense that is not vile); one (absence of both vileness and self-defense); or two (vile murder unrelated to self-defense).

Thus, the Barnett System has 18 possible classifications (3x2x3); the higher the summation score on the three dimensions, the more aggravated the case. For example, the least culpable case would be scored as (0,0,0), and the most as (2,1,2). The Barnett System classifies cases into six categories on the basis of their summation scores. The six categories include scores ranging from 0 to 4. This allows cases with specific fact patterns to be grouped and compared to other cases with disparate circumstances. For example, Case A (1,0,1) is classified with Case B (1,1,0) into category 2 (cases with severity scores of two). These cases are more aggravated than Case C (1,0,0) and Case D (0,0,1), which are grouped together into category 1 (cases with severity scores of one).

Using this system, Barnett (1985) found that 25 percent of the category 3 scores resulted in a death sentence and 78 percent of the category 4 and up cases resulted in a death sentence. Only 11 percent (5 out of 45) of the black victim cases in category 3 resulted in death sentences in comparison to 32 percent (28 out of 89) of the white victim cases (Barnett, 1985, p. 1350).

In support of the "liberation hypothesis", the race effects within this category were most pronounced in the (1,1,1) cases. These cases were scored as average in terms of certainty and deliberateness. The victims were strangers, and the killings were not vile or in self-defense. There were 20 white victim (1,1,1) cases, ten of which resulted in death. However, of the 11 black victim cases, only one resulted in death. It is important to note that Barnett (1985) did not look at multiple decision points. As a result, it is impossible to determine when race was most likely to have an impact.

Gross and Mauro (1984) examined sentencing in eight states: Arkansas, Florida, Georgia, Illinois, Mississippi, North Carolina, Oklahoma, and Virginia. Data were collected from Supplementary Homicide Reports on all homicides reported to the FBI from 1976 to

1980. A total of 379 death sentences (one-third of the nation's total at the time) were included in the study. The researchers controlled for sex of the suspected killer; the sex, age and race of the victim; the date and location of the homicide; the weapon used; contemporaneous felony; and the relationship between the victim and suspected killer. Data on those on death row were collected from Death Row U.S.A., which included race of the defendant, the race of the victim, the sex of the victim, the use of a gun, the commission of a separate felony in conjunction with the homicide, the number of victims, the relationship of the defendant to the victim, and the location of the homicide.

Felony circumstances, defendant/victim relationship, and the number of victims were found to be the most important legal predictors of capital sentencing in Florida, Georgia, and Illinois. An aggravation scale encompassing these three variables was used to estimate the effects of race on sentencing within these three states. The presence or absence of each factor was scored, so that four levels of aggravation were created (0,1,2,3). A score of 0 indicated that none of the factors were present, and a score of 3 indicated that all three were present. The level of aggravation did not account for the race-of-victim effects in Florida, Georgia, or Illinois.

Black-defendant/white-victim cases resulted in higher rates of death penalties than black-defendant/black-victim cases within every level of aggravation (except category 0 in Georgia). These disparities ranged from 2 to 40 percentage points. The most stable discrepancies appeared to be in level 2 where there were at least 41 cases in both racial categories. The disparity was 40 percentage points in Georgia, 24 in Florida, and 8 in Illinois. A similar pattern was found when the researchers collapsed the categories into white victim and black victim cases. In level 1, white victim cases were twice as likely to result in a death sentence than black victim cases in Georgia, five times more likely in Florida, and six times more likely in Illinois.

Gross and Mauro (1984) reported that the discrepancies were largest in the most aggravated cases. When collapsing levels 2 and 3 into one level of aggravation, the sentencing rates were 47% for white victim cases and 4% for black victim cases in Georgia, 28 vs. 8 in Florida, and 12 vs. 4 in Illinois. It is important to note that the researchers did not look at race effects at various decision points, e.g., jury sentencing.

Gross and Mauro (1984) also used a regression analysis to look at race effects. After controlling for all of the legal factors in their dataset, the killing of a white victim increased the odds of a death sentence by an estimated factor of four in Illinois, five in Florida, and about seven in Georgia.

John McAdams' (1998) reanalysis of the Gross and Mauro (1984) data found that all three aggravating factors had to be present in a black/black homicide before the probability of a death sentence was comparable to the odds in a black/white homicide with two factors. In addition, the race of the defendant did not have a significant effect after controlling for the race of the victim. McAdams went on to state that "there is a general and quite robust bias against black victims, and there is no general bias against black defendants," (McAdams, 1998, p. 166).

Sorensen and Wallace (1995) identified the population of death eligible cases from 1977 to 1991 in Missouri using Supplementary Homicide Reports. Of the universe of 3,873 non-negligent homicide arrests, 353 were convicted of capital murder. The pool of death eligible cases was further limited to arrests involving a contemporaneous felony. Data on capital murders resulting in conviction were obtained from trial judge reports. Three decision points were analyzed: charge/conviction, penalty trial, and sentencing. Sorensen and Wallace created an aggravation scale for each decision point and looked at race effects within each level. The researchers controlled for 31 variables including mitigating and aggravating factors.

An aggravation scale was created using a logistic regression model. Five variables were found in the analysis to be significant predictors of sentence outcome—prior violent record, prison killing, weapon, relationship, and non-statutory aggravating factors. A culpability score was assigned to a given case by summing the non-standardized beta coefficients from the regression that corresponded to each factor present in the case.

The researchers found that race was not a factor in the most aggravated cases. However, at the lowest level of aggravation, cases involving white victims were nearly twice as likely to result in a death sentence than those involving black victims. The death sentence rate was 2 ½ times higher in the black-defendant/white-victim category than in the black-defendant/black-victim category (Sorensen & Wallace, 1995, p. 77).

The preeminent studies on race and sentencing were conducted by Baldus, Woodworth and Pulaski and were admitted into evidence in *McCleskey v. Kemp* (1987). The evidence presented encompassed two studies: the Procedural Reform Study (PRS), undertaken in 1979, and the Charging and Sentencing Study (CSS), which was completed in 1980. Race-of-defendant was not found to be a significant factor in the post-*Furman* system in Georgia; however, it did seem to play a role when the data from the state were broken down regionally. White defendants were disadvantaged in urban areas and black defendants in rural areas. The race-of-victim was found to have an effect on prosecutorial discretion and jury sentencing decisions.

A large scale linear multiple regression analysis found that after adjusting for 163 variables the only aggravating circumstance with more explanatory power than the race-of-victim variable was the number of statutory aggravating circumstances present in the case. The status of the victim was also found to be a significant predictor of sentencing outcomes.

The Procedural Reform Study (PRS) included 594 offenders who were arrested, prosecuted for murder, and sentenced by a jury to life or death between 1973 and 1978. Out of 206 penalty trials, the jury imposed the death sentence 112 times. Baldus et al. (1990) collected data on 150 aggravating and mitigating factors from a multitude of sources. The study looked at two decision points: the prosecutor's decision to seek the death penalty after a jury convicts, and the jury's decision to impose a life or death sentence.

The PRS used both *a priori* and empirical methods to classify cases. The legislative criteria (*a priori*) postulates that the blameworthiness of an offender varies as a function of the number of statutorily designated aggravating circumstances present in the case. The second *a priori* method ranked each case on the basis of the number and importance of the aggravating and mitigating factors present. Evaluators read summaries of every case and identified the aggravating and mitigating factors present, weighed the factors against each other, and categorized them into five levels of culpability. Cases were then ranked within each culpability level. The rankings were compared and disagreements worked out by consensus. A multiple regression analysis (empirical) was used to identify the factors that best explained sentencing outcomes. Each case was scored by summing the beta coefficients of each factor present. Cases were then ranked, and sorted into six culpability categories.

The odds of receiving a death sentence for the average defendant whose victim was white were found to be 4.3 times greater than a defendant whose victim was black under similar circumstances after adjusting for 23 non-racial case characteristics (Baldus et al., 1990, p. 154). Results from the regression-based index of culpability indicated a 15-percentage point race disparity in jury sentence outcomes. Consistent with the "liberation hypothesis," these disparities were most pronounced in the mid-aggravation level cases where the death sentence rate was below .80 (Baldus et al., 1990, p. 163).

Race-of-victim effects were strongest in cases with no mitigating evidence. There was also a strong correlation between victim-based discrimination and number of statutory aggravators. The level of violence appeared to be more important in white victim cases, and mitigating factors related to drugs and alcohol were more important in black victim cases. Finally, murder motivated by race hatred was treated as a strong aggravating factor when the victim was white, but had a mitigating effect when he or she was black (Baldus et al., 1990, p. 172).

The Charging and Sentencing Study included cases spanning from 1973 to 1979 in which defendants were arrested and charged with homicide and subsequently convicted of murder or voluntary manslaughter. A stratified random sample of 1,066 cases was drawn from a universe of 2,484 cases. The final sample included more than 300 jury trial murder convictions, and 127 death sentences. Data were collected on over 230 variables. The CSS examined five decision points: grand jury indictment, prosecutorial plea-bargain, jury conviction, decision to move ahead with the penalty phase, and jury sentence.

Baldus et al. (1990) used a triangulation approach, which used both *a priori* and empirical methods to classify cases. Three *a priori* measures were used. The first subdivided cases into four groups based on the presence or absence of either felony circumstances or a serious prior record. The second measure identified murder cases in the sample that were committed during the commission of a felony, and as a result were death eligible. These cases were sorted according to the nature of the contemporaneous felony. Only armed robbery cases had a sufficient sample size to allow for further categorization. The armed robbery cases were subdivided into seven additional categories according to the nature of other contemporaneous offenses that may have been present. The third *a priori* measure used a coding protocol developed by a judge and former prosecutor. An empirical method was also employed that used a linear regression to determine which case characteristics best explained observed sentencing outcomes.

Like in the Procedural Reform Study, race-of-victim disparities were found to be concentrated in the midlevel aggravation cases, consistent with the "liberation hypothesis." Race-of-victim disparities were between 20 to 30 percentage points (Baldus et al., 1990, p. 323). Results from the analyses on the effects of race-of-victim on jury decisions were equivocal. A linear analysis that controlled for all statistically significant background factors resulted in a weak race-of-victim effect that was not significant. However, a similar analysis using logistic procedures produced an odds multiplier of 3.4 that was significant (Baldus et al., 1990, p. 327).

As discussed in the previous chapter, the Supreme Court chose to dismiss these findings as suggestive at best. Although the "Baldus Study" uncovered a significant pattern of racial disparities within the capital system in Georgia, this research, like the archival literature as a whole fails to address how race affects sentencing. Baldus, Woodworth, Zuckerman, Weiner, and Broffitt (1998) attempted to address this limitation in a study on the capital system in Philadelphia.

The Philadelphia study's sample pool included all death-eligible defendants between 1989 and 1993. Three decision points were examined: 1) the finding of a statutory aggravating circumstance; (2) the finding of a mitigating factor; and (3) the weighing of statutory aggravation and mitigation. The final sample of 524 death eligible cases included 118 death sentences, 230 life sentences, and 176 non-penalty trial cases.

The researchers used an inferential procedure to quantify the strength of evidence for the statutory aggravating and mitigating circumstances presented in each case. This allowed them to explore the impact of race and/or deathworthiness on the finding of aggravating and mitigating circumstances. Evidence supporting the aggravating factors was classified on a four-point scale, and evidence supporting mitigating circumstances on a three-point scale.

Four different culpability measures were used to classify cases, the first being the legislative procedure. The second method—the salient factor measure—classified cases by the primary aggravating factor(s) and then by the other relevant statutory aggravating and mitigating circumstances present in the case. The third measure was a severity index based on the results of a murder severity study where respondents ranked a small group of cases in terms of culpability, and the fourth method used a multiple logistic regression technique.

Pennsylvania differs from other states in that a jury that fails to find at least one mitigating factor[9] present during the sentencing phase must return a death sentence.[10] Over one-half of all death sentences imposed in Pennsylvania fall within this category. If a mitigating factor(s) is found to be present, then the jury is instructed to weigh the aggravating factor(s) against the mitigating factor(s).

A regression analysis indicated that the race-of-victim variable had a significant effect on the odds that a jury found a mitigating factor. The race-of-defendant variable had a significant effect on the weighing process after a mitigator was found. Consistent with the "liberation hypothesis," these effects were most pronounced in the midrange cases in terms of culpability.

A logistic regression was also used to classify cases into six culpability levels. Death sentence rates were estimated for the two racial groups within each level. A nine- percentage point race-of-victim

---

[9] This requires the affirmative vote of only one juror.

[10] This system of mandatory death sentences passed judicial scrutiny in *Blystone v. Pennsylvania* (1990) (494 U.S. 299). The statute reads as follows:

> (iii) aggravating circumstances must be proved by the Commonwealth beyond a reasonable doubt; mitigating circumstances must be proved by the defendant by a preponderance of the evidence
> (iv) the verdict must be a sentence of death if the jury unanimously finds at least one aggravating circumstance specified in subsection (d) and no mitigating circumstance or if the jury unanimously finds one or more aggravating circumstances which outweigh any mitigating circumstances. The verdict must be a sentence of life imprisonment in all other cases.

disparity was found in the failure to find a mitigator category, and a 21-percentage point race-of-defendant disparity was found in the weighing category. Both findings were significant (Baldus et al., 1998, p. 1695). These patterns were consistent across several different classification systems, e.g., the salient factor measure.

Baldus et al. (1998) also looked at the effects of race on the finding of specific types of mitigating circumstances. Juries were less likely to find the age mitigating factor or the catchall mitigating factor when the victim was not black.[11] When the evidence supported the age factor, juries found it present 38 percent of the time in non-black victim cases and 74 percent of the time in black victim cases. When the evidence supported the catchall factor, it was found in 46 percent of the non-black victim cases and in 64 percent of the black victim cases (Baldus et al., 1998, p. 1719).

This study attempted to address the limitations imposed on archival research and examine how race affects the evaluation of evidence. The results suggest that the race of the victim and the race of the defendant have different effects on sentencing in Philadelphia. The victim's race was found to affect the likelihood that juries found a mitigating factor present. Juries were less likely to find a mitigator when the victim was white. Mitigators that were found had little influence in the weighing process. What influence they did have was moderated by the race of the defendant. For example, the catchall factor appeared to be given no weight in the black defendant cases, but had a considerable impact in the non-black defendant cases (Baldus et al., 1998, p. 1721). Thus, juries were less likely to find a mitigator when the victim was white, and gave it more weight when the defendant was not black. These race effects were strongest in the midrange cases of culpability. This implies that a complicated relationship exists between race and sentencing in Philadelphia that is mediated by the evaluation of mitigating evidence, and moderated by the strength of the evidence.

---

[11] These are two statutory mitigating factors in Pennsylvania: under 18 years of age at time of the crime, and anything proffered by the defendant that does not fall within the other statutory defined mitigating categories. It is interesting to note that the age factor is not a subjective mitigator. It is peculiar that race affected the finding of such a factor.

The archival research on the post-*Furman* capital system documents a pattern of race-of-victim discrimination within each stage of the process, beginning with the prosecution's decision to bring capital charges (see Sorensen et al., 2001; GAO, 1988; Keil & Vito, 1995) and concluding with the jury's sentencing recommendation or decision (e.g., Keil & Vito, 1995). Black-defendant/white-victim homicide has been shown to be far more likely to result in a death sentence than black-defendant/black-victim homicide. Studies that have controlled for the deathworthiness of cases have mostly found evidence in support of the "liberation hypothesis." Race effects are strongest in the low-to-moderate aggravation level cases when the evidence is ambiguous and sentence decision unclear. This finding suggests that white jurors are not likely to display discriminatory behavior in situations where they cannot justify their decisions with race-neutral explanations. This is consistent with the aversive racism perspective, and must be accounted for in a model of juror sentencing. The Baldus et al. (1998) study was the only attempt to go beyond the examination of sentence outcomes and look at the process by which race effects occur. The race of the defendant was found to have an impact on how mitigating evidence was evaluated. Thus, it is possible that a race-of-defendant effect exists, but that the archival methodology is not able to detect it. This issue will be explored in Chapter 5.

LIMITATIONS TO THE ARCHIVAL STUDIES

Although the external validity of the archival research is buttressed by the very nature of the data, a myriad of criticisms have been raised in court decisions and by experts concerning the internal validity and conclusions drawn from this body of literature. Four of these criticisms stand out: sample selection bias; small sample sizes; the failure to include the entire gamut of decision-making points; and the failure to control for legitimate case factors (GAO, 1990, p. 3).

Sample selection bias arises when the sample of cases selected for examination is the result of discretionary decisions made at earlier points in the criminal justice system (Gross & Mauro, 1984, p. 46). A sample drawn from the universe of cases that reach a sentencing hearing is affected by decisions made at the earlier stages of the process, e.g., the prosecutor's decision to file capital charges. Discrimination in the earlier stages may mask or minimize racial patterns at the latter stages of the process. For example, it is possible that cases involving the killing of blacks that make it to the sentencing stage are more seriously aggravated than cases involving the killing of whites. If this occurs, race-of-victim effects at later stages may appear to be weak, in that both white and black victim homicides result in similar sentences. However, under these circumstances, killers of whites would effectively be sentenced to death for less serious crimes than killers of blacks. Researchers may erroneously conclude that there are no race effects if attention is not paid to decisions made at the early points in the process. Sample selection bias is most likely to be a factor in studies that look at the final sentence outcome, or only at jury-sentencing decisions, and is least likely to be a factor in studies that examine the population of all reported homicides. Many of the earlier studies on the post-*Furman* system failed to account for sample selection bias.

The second criticism relates to insufficient sample size (see McAdams, 1998). The majority of homicides do not result in capital murder indictments. Death sentences are even less frequent. As a result, a large sample is required to examine the effects of race on later decision points. A vast number of the archival studies do not have a sufficient number of death sentences in their sample to examine race effects on jury decisions after controlling for legal case factors.

The third criticism focuses on the failure to look at the effects of race on each decision point (see Weitzer, 1996). There are four discretionary decision points: the decision to indict for a death eligible crime; the decision to offer a plea bargain; the jury's verdict at the guilt phase; and the jury's final sentencing decision. Studies that look at overall race effects cannot identify the point(s) where race is likely to have an impact, or the magnitude of the effect at each decision point.

Finally, both valid and invalid criticisms have arisen concerning the number of legal case factors that some of these studies have taken into account. Criticisms are legitimate when a study fails to control for case factors that are correlated with race and sentencing (see Kleck, 1985). Without controlling for these factors, it is not possible to rule them out as explanations for observed racial disparities. Criticisms become suspect when studies with a high level of control are criticized for ignoring variables that are theoretically unlikely to be related to race and sentencing. Although these factors must be taken into account when evaluating the quality of the various archival studies on race and sentencing in the post-*Furman* system, as a whole, this large body of research has uncovered a consistent trend across sentencing schemes that is difficult to discount.

CHAPTER 3

THE POST-TRIAL INTERVIEW RESEARCH ON RACE AND SENTENCING

The Baldus et al. (1998) piece is the only archival study that attempted to look at the decision-making process. The results of that study suggest that both the race of the defendant and the race of the victim affect sentencing, but in different capacities. The idiosyncrasy in the Pennsylvania capital sentencing system prescribes a death sentence when juries unanimously determine that no mitigating factors exist. Juries tended to perceive non-black victim cases to be more aggravated than black victim cases and were more likely to exercise this mechanism when the victim was not black. In addition, jurors tended to reject the excuses (mitigation) provided by black defendants, while giving the same excuses mitigating weight when the defendant was not black.

Evidence from some of the post-trial questionnaire literature also tends to show that the race of the victim and the race of the defendant have an effect on jurors' sentencing decisions. White jurors appear to be more punitive when the victim is white, and perceive black defendants to be more dangerous than white defendants. These effects are consistent with a victim evaluation and defendant attribution process. The survey data also suggest that the composition of the jury moderates the effect that race has on final sentencing decisions in black-defendant/white-victim homicides. Like the strength of the evidence, the deliberations process in confluence with the composition of the jury may have an influence on the normative structure of the sentencing task. The salience of white jurors' egalitarian values and race-based norms may be enhanced when racial tension is brought to the forefront during the deliberations. This has been shown to be most likely to occur when a black male is sitting on the jury. The data also indicate that many jurors reach a sentencing decision either before the penalty phase or penalty deliberations begin. This suggests that jurors are relying upon their own decision rules, rather than on the instructions provided by the judge to reach a sentencing position.

THE CAPITAL JURY PROJECT

Extensive open- and close-ended interviews with capital jurors have been conducted in an effort to gain some insight into the decision-making process. The Capital Jury Project has interviewed over 1,100 capital jurors from 340 trials that have made it to the sentencing phase in fourteen states. An attempt was made to randomly sample four jurors from each case. Data were collected on some 700 variables via extensive three-to-four hour post-trial interviews with each juror. This represents the largest single effort to study the processes that jurors and juries undergo when deciding upon sentence.

During the course of the interview, jurors were asked to recall what they thought the punishment should have been at four different points. They were asked to recall what their sentencing position was: (1) after the guilt decision but before the sentencing stage of the trial; (2) after the judge's sentencing instructions but before deliberations; (3) at the first jury vote on punishment; and (4) at the final punishment vote.

It is important to note that this type of recall task is susceptible to hindsight bias, particularly when the time lapse between the trial and the recall task is significant. Research has shown that people tend to report prior positions that are consistent with the final outcome. Fischhoff (1975) found that voters reconstructed their retrospective reports of their votes to be consistent with the final election results. If jurors cannot retrieve their prior sentence positions from memory, they may utilize the outcome information they do have, i.e., sentence decision, as an anchor for estimating those positions (Stahlberg & Maass, 1998). If the hindsight bias was affecting jurors' recall of their sentencing positions, these self-reports would likely be consistent with the final outcome. This was not the case. As indicated below, there was variation between each measurement point. This is inconsistent with the hindsight bias effect.

Using data from the Capital Jury Project, Bowers, Steiner, and Sandys (2001) looked at the effects of race and gender on both jury and juror decision-making. Of the 340 cases in the sample, 74 were black-defendant/white-victim cases and 60 were black-defendant/black-victim cases. The archival literature has shown that racial disparities are largest between these two categories. A sub-sample was drawn from these 134 cases that included only those where both black and white jurors were interviewed. This sub-sample included 23 black-defendant/white-victim cases and 13 black-defendant/black-victim cases. These 40 cases were used for the analysis on the effects of juror race on decision-making within these two categories.

Under certain conditions, victim evaluations may be affected by the race of the juror and the race of the victim. There is anecdotal evidence that jurors evaluated victims who were members of their own racial group more positively than victims who were members of a different racial category. These tendencies were reflected in the analysis from the sub-sample on jurors' sentencing positions.

The effects of race on victim evaluations should be most pronounced in interracial homicide. In the black-defendant/white-victim category, the majority of white jurors leaned towards death and the majority of black jurors towards life. This contrast appeared in the early stages and continued to develop until the first sentencing vote. [12] By the first vote, the two racial groups were polarized. Over 67 percent

[12] This description only includes the first three measurement points; thus, the final punishment vote is excluded. There are several reasons for this decision. First, the final sentence vote should reflect the final sentence outcome in the majority of the cases. This is because all but a few states require a unanimous verdict. As a result, jurors' final votes will be identical in a given case. Second, there are too many events that can occur between the third (first vote) and the final measurement points. For example, there is no way of knowing how many votes took place between the two points.

of white jurors were in favor of death, and over 69 percent of black jurors in favor of life. This suggests that white jurors perceived a white victim homicide to be more deserving of death than did black jurors.

Jurors' sentencing positions in the black-defendant/black-victim category also support a victim evaluation process that is affected by race. Unlike black jurors in the black/white category who tended to take a life sentence position, the majority of black jurors in the black/black category supported a death sentence. This majority increased at each stage of the process culminating in the first sentence vote.

When both the defendant and victim were black, white jurors tended to show a level of ambivalence, which was reflected in their sentencing positions. In this condition, they were less punitive than black jurors. White jurors in the black/black category were also much less likely to lean towards death than white jurors in the black/white category, and were also more likely to remain undecided at each of the three punishment points.

These findings suggest that jurors of both races, within black-defendant/white-victim and black-defendant/black-victim cases, tend to take early death sentence stances when the victim is of the same race. This comports with the research on inter-group conflict. It is plausible that jurors in these categories were identifying with their respective in-group and acting accordingly. Thus, group membership on the premise of race may mediate the relationship between victim race and victim evaluations. This will be developed in Chapter 5.

Evidence from Bowers et al. (2001) also suggests that the defendant attribution process is affected by the race of the defendant. Although the researchers did not measure attributions directly, they did measure jurors' perceptions of future dangerousness. Future dangerousness can be conceptualized as a negative internal attribution in that it indicates that the murder was perceived to be a product of a stable cause that is likely to result in further violence. Results from the analysis on the entire sample of 340 cases, which included both life and death sentences, indicate that white jurors were more likely to make a negative internal attribution, and perceive the evidence to be consistent with that attribution when the defendant was black than when he was white.

Approximately 89 percent of white jurors in the black defendant/white-victim condition and 89 percent of the white jurors in the black-defendant/black-victim condition thought that "dangerous to other people" described the defendant "fairly" or "very well." In addition, they perceived the evidence to be consistent with that attribution in both black defendant categories. Approximately 85 percent of white jurors in the black-defendant/white-victim condition and 86 percent in the black/black condition thought that the evidence proved that the defendant would be dangerous in the future. This finding did not vary as a function of the victim's race. This suggests that the race of the victim does not have an effect on the defendant attribution process. White jurors were also less likely to make a negative internal attribution for a white defendant's behavior.

White defendants were more likely than black defendants to be described by white jurors as "sorry" and less likely to be described as "dangerous to other people." In addition, whitc jurors were less likely to believe that the evidence proved that a white defendant would be dangerous in the future. In the white-defendant/white-victim condition, 72 percent of white jurors agreed that the evidence proved that the defendant would be dangerous in the future, as compared to approximately 85 percent in the black defendant conditions.

Bowers et al. (2001) also looked at the effects of jury composition on sentence outcomes. It is possible that black jurors will address race during deliberations resulting in the activation of norms admonishing against discriminatory behavior. This is particularly likely to occur in interracial homicide. The composition of the jury may affect the salience of white jurors' egalitarian ideals, moderating the effects of race on sentencing. Juries in the black-defendant/white-victim category with five or more white males were more likely to return a death sentence than those with four or less. There was a 40-point percentage disparity in death sentencing rates between juries with four and those with five white males.

The presence of a black male juror reduced the odds of a death sentence. Death sentences were imposed in 72 percent of the cases without a black male on the jury and 43 percent in the cases with at least one. The researchers labeled these two patterns the "white male dominance" effect and the "black male presence" effect (Bowers et al., 2001, p. 193). There were no composition effects in the intra-racial categories. This may be the result of ambivalence on the part of white jurors towards black-on-black crime, or the absence of racial conflict between white and black jurors.

The "black male presence" effect is consistent with the hypothesis laid out above. Black males may activate white jurors' egalitarian values during deliberations, attenuating the relationship between white jurors' internal pre-deliberation positions, which may have been affected by race, and their final explicit sentence votes. Likewise, the presence of five or more white jurors may increase the likelihood that prejudice will remain beneath the surface; reducing the odds that race-based sentencing will be suppressed. It is important to note that the researchers did not control for the strength of the evidence. As a result, alternative explanations to the jury composition hypothesis for these disparities cannot be ruled out. It is possible, for example, that cases with at least one black male were less aggravated than cases with five or more white males.

Bowers et al.'s (2001) data provide some support for the hypothesis that jurors make victim evaluative and defendant attribution judgments. Race appears to have an independent effect on these two processes. In addition, the composition of the jury has been shown to reduce the effects of race at the later stages of the deliberations process.

Evidence from the Capital Jury Project's data has also shown that jurors tend to arrive at punishment decisions before hearing the sentencing instructions (see Bowers, Sandys, & Steiner, 1998). This suggests that jurors are relying on their own decision rules, not the guidance from the court, to reach a sentence position. The focus of the evidence in the sentence phase on the blameworthiness of the defendant and the value of the victim's life enhances the likelihood that these decision rules will be based on victim evaluations and defendant attributions. If this is the case, jurors are using the type of heuristic process that was admonished against by the *Booth* Court. That is, defendants whose victims were assets to their community are perceived to be more deserving of punishment than those whose victims were perceived to be less worthy.

Bowers, Sandys, and Steiner (1998) used data from the Capital Jury Project on 916 jurors from 11 states to look at jurors' likelihood of taking an early sentence position. It was found that early sentencing positions were related to final sentencing decisions. Over 48 percent of jurors reported that they thought they knew what the punishment should be during the guilt phase of the trial (Bowers et al, 1998, p. 1488). In addition, only 19 percent of those that took an early death penalty stance and 13 percent of those who took a life stance reported to have shifted their sentence positions at the end of the proceeding. Thus, early sentencing positions appear to be resilient. Finally, over 60 percent of the jurors who took an early sentence position were absolutely convinced on the proper sentence. This number increased to over 64 percent for those reported to have reached a sentence decision after the penalty trial but before deliberations. Jurors' confidence in their early positions, which appear to be unlikely to change over the course of the trial, implies that they either perceived the sentence phase evidence to support their positions, or discounted evidence that suggested an alternative outcome. Research has shown that there is a tendency to make a cognitive effort to disconfirm evidence that is inconsistent with a prior held attitude or belief (e.g., Edwards & Smith, 1996). Overall, these data imply that jurors are likely to rely on their own decision rules, not the instruction provided by the court, to reach a sentencing position. In addition, these positions appear to be resilient to disconfirmatory evidence.

LIMITATIONS TO THE POST-TRIAL INTERVIEW RESEARCH

Although this field method has obvious benefits, i.e., real jurors, it also has some serious drawbacks. Self-reports are open to certain types of bias, e.g., impression management. "Jurors may try to present themselves in a flattering light, overestimate their own influence on the group, or experience self-enhancing memory distortions," (Costanzo & Costanzo, 1992, p. 190). In addition, people are not always aware of all the factors that influenced their decisions (see Nisbett & Wilson, 1977), or willing to disclose the use of illegitimate factors. Thus, their reports may not be accurate representations of what occurred.

As discussed previously, jurors' self-reports can be affected by hindsight bias, altering their memories so that they are consistent with the final sentence decision. A juror may report that the mitigating evidence was weak and did not play a significant role in her sentencing decision. This may be an accurate assessment, or she may have reconstructed the memory to be consistent with the final sentence outcome. Although these drawbacks must be taken into account when evaluating the post-trial interview data, the interview can provide a rich source of information about how a decision was made (see Ericcson & Simon, 1980).

The experimental method provides an opportunity to control for many of the variables that limit the findings from the field research discussed in the previous two chapters (e.g., hindsight bias, and case severity). However, like the field research, this methodology is also open to various criticisms.

CHAPTER 4

THE EXPERIMENTAL RESEARCH ON RACE AND SENTENCING

The archival method is the strongest technique—with respect to external validity—for identifying disparities in sentence outcomes in the capital system and when they are most likely to occur. However, this type of research, with the exception of Baldus et al. (1998) does not offer much insight into how or why these disparities occur, or how race impacts prosecutor, juror, and judicial sentencing decisions. The post-trial interview data do provide some insight into the decision-making process; however, this method relies on jurors' recall, which can be subject to error. The experimental literature on sentencing, which has been labeled "mock jury" research, is a third body of research that has been employed in an attempt to shed some light onto how race affects the evaluation of information and sentence positions. Although the external validity of this research is a matter of debate, the laboratory does offer a controlled setting where data can be collected and evaluation processes examined in a fashion that the archival and post-trial methods cannot provide.

As discussed in Chapter 2, there is strong support in the archival data for a race-of-victim effect. However, the evidence in support of a race-of-defendant effect is equivocal. In some studies, an offender effect was found. At times this variable was shown to interact with other variables (e.g., region and/or victim race) and at other times, it was shown to vary in direction. In contrast, the experimental literature on sentencing has found a consistent race-of-offender effect, but has failed to replicate the race-of-victim effect.

WHAT DOES THE LABORATORY RESEARCH TELL US

The decision-making task in the sentencing phase of a capital trial requires each juror to answer an attribution question. Unlike the determination of guilt, this task is subjective in nature. Jurors are now asked to evaluate the gravity of the crime, and then determine the blameworthiness or cause of the defendant's behavior and, in some states, the future danger he or she poses to society. Internal attribution styles have been shown to have an effect on participants' sentence recommendations (see Cochran, Boots, & Heide, 2003). In addition, race has been shown to have an influence on these types of attribution tasks. However, these effects appear to occur only under specific circumstances.

Mazzella and Feingold (1994) conducted a meta-analysis using studies that examined a variety of types of crimes. This analysis included over eighty studies on the effects of physical attractiveness, race, socioeconomic status, and gender on participants' judgments of guilt and recommended punishment. Although there were no overall effects of race on judgments, the effect of race-of-defendant on punishment was found to be moderated by crime type. Participants recommended greater punishment for negligent homicide when the defendant was black and for fraud when the defendant was white (Mazzella & Feingold, 1994, p. 1332). This pattern suggests that crimes that are assumed to be stereotypical of particular races may elicit harsher punishments in comparison to crimes that are inconsistent with a given racial stereotype. However, studies have also shown that this relationship is attenuated by the salience of participants' egalitarian values and the clarity of the sentencing task.

In a study conducted by Gordon (1990), participants perceived a black burglar's behavior as being more due to personality characteristics than was the behavior of the black embezzler. Burglary was perceived as being a more typical crime for a black defendant than was embezzlement, and the black burglar was judged more likely than the black embezzler to commit a similar crime in the future. The extent to which the offender's behavior was attributed to race resulted in a crime-type/offender-race interaction for black participants. Black participants viewed race as a more significant factor for the white embezzler than for the white burglar. This interaction was not significant for white study participants. Consistent with this finding, significant positive correlations were found between jail sentences and the extent to which black participants felt offender race was a factor responsible for the individual committing the crime. Positive correlations were also found, for black participants, between punishment and the tendency to form dispositional attributions regarding the offender's behavior.

The significance of the crime-type/offender-race interaction found by Gordon (1990) appears to have been moderated by participant race: Black participants' attributions were affected by crime type, but white participants were not. This suggests that race-based attributions are not robust. However, there are aspects of the study's methodology that offer an alternative explanation. The questionnaire used by Gordon asked participants to what extent they believed that several factors, including race, might have been responsible for the defendant's crime. This type of questioning may have activated white jurors' egalitarian norms and attenuated the influence of stereotypes on their behavior. Thus, race-based stereotypes may only affect white jurors' attributions when they are not cognizant of the racial aspect of the attribution task. Black participants' behavior may be less susceptible to the influences of the egalitarian value system.

In a national survey of adults over 18, Chiricos, Welch, and Gertz (2004) found that the racial typification of a crime had a significant effect on respondents' sentencing recommendations. However, like Gordon (1990), this was moderated by race. Specifically, this relationship was only significant for white participants.

Sommers and Ellsworth (2000) tested aversive racism as a theoretical explanation for the differences between white and black participants' attributions and punishment decisions in interracial crimes where racial tension was salient. In their first study, offender race influenced white and black participants differently. Offender race did not have an effect on white participants' punishment recommendations.

However, black participants recommended significantly harsher punishment for white than for black defendants. The same pattern was found for participants' dispositional attributions for behavior. These disparities between white and black participants are consistent with Gordon's (1990) findings. The second study by Sommers and Ellsworth manipulated the salience of racial tension by using an interracial crime scenario that either included or excluded the presence of a racial slur. The race salient condition results were similar to those in the first study. However, results in the non-race salient condition supported an aversive racism hypothesis. Both white and black participants were more punitive toward the different race offender. A similar pattern of bias was found for negative dispositional attributions.

Race-of-offender effects may be influenced by the salience of external norms proscribing discriminatory behavior for white participants. These norms are likely to become salient when the crime in question encompasses a characteristic that evokes racial tension, e.g., a racial slur. Research has also shown that instruction comprehension, a variable that provides structure to the sentencing task, attenuates the effects of offender race on sentencing positions.

Lynch and Haney (2000) looked at the effects of offender and victim race on punishment decisions in situations where instruction comprehension was poor and evidence ambiguous. Jury eligible citizens who were either registered to vote or licensed to drive in California completed a death penalty questionnaire to determine their eligibility to serve as a juror under death qualification standards. Participants viewed an abridged version of a capital penalty trial that was pretested and adjusted so that it was neither so aggravated nor so mitigated that participants would vote overwhelming for either verdict choice. Thus, the evidence was ambiguous. The race of the victim and offender were varied orthogonally so that there were four different versions of the trial. Participants were then read standard California death penalty instructions, supplied with a copy, and instructed to complete a verdict form and questionnaire.

There were no significant main effects for the race-of-victim variable on punishment, or any significant interrelationships between comprehension, victim race, and punishment. However, there was a significant main effect for race of the offender on punishment. Several interactions were also found to have significant effects on punishment, including the interaction between high/low instruction comprehension and offender race. When comprehension was low, participants were more likely to sentence black offenders than white offenders to death. When it was high, race did not have an effect on punishment (Lynch & Haney, 2000, p. 349). The interaction between punishment, comprehension, and the offender/victim race condition was also significant. When comprehension was low, participants in the black-offender/white-victim condition sentenced the offender to death at a higher rate than participants in the white-offender/black-victim condition, (Lynch & Haney, 2000, p. 351). These findings suggest that the instructions affect the likelihood that participants will refer to race-based heuristics and decision rules when making a sentencing decision. When instruction comprehension is high, the sentencing task is less ambiguous; thus, participants are limited by the instructions, which provide guidance. However, when instruction comprehension is low, the task is unclear. Under these conditions, participants are likely to resort to heuristic decision rules and judgment processes in their effort to reach a sentencing decision.

Lynch and Haney's (2000) results coupled with those of Sommers and Ellsworth (2000), suggest that the effects of race on sentencing are moderated by factors that govern the development of the normative structure within the sentencing task; affect the availability of nonracial factors that can be used to rationalize race-based sentencing; and enhance the salience of societal norms admonishing against discriminatory behavior. When racial tension is not in the forefront, jury instructions are unclear, and the sentencing phase evidence is ambiguous, there is no clear structure guiding the decision-making task or inhibiting discriminatory sentencing. Under these conditions, jurors are likely to resort to heuristic processes to reach a sentence decision In addition, jurors' egalitarian ideals are not likely to attenuate the influence of race on these decisions. A theory of race and sentencing must take into account variables (e.g., instruction comprehension) that have an influence on the development of the normative structure in the sentencing task and affect the activation of norms governing behavior (e.g., black males on the jury).

The race of the offender influences attributions when the crime is consistent with a given stereotype. The meta-analysis conducted by Mazzella and Feingold (1994) supports this supposition; race effects were moderated by crime type. Bodenhausen and Wyer (1985) tested a heuristic model in an attempt to determine how and when race is likely to affect attributions in a sentencing task. According to the heuristic hypothesis:

> People use stereotypes as a heuristic in interpreting the behavior of others and that they search for alternative interpretations only if a stereotype-based interpretation is inapplicable. If the transgression is stereotypical of the offender's group, the stereotype will be used to interpret the behavior and make punishment recommendations regardless of whether other information with different implications is available (Bodenhausen & Wyer, 1985, p. 268).

Bodenhausen and Wyer (1985) found support for the heuristic hypothesis. In their second experiment, participants made parole recommendations for offenders convicted of different types of crimes. The name of the offender was used to manipulate the activation of the stereotype and its consistency with the crime. Participants judged a crime to be more stable, recommending harsher punishment when it was consistent with the activated stereotype, and less-stable, recommending leniency when the crime was inconsistent with the activated stereotype (Bodenhausen & Wyer, 1985, p. 276).

Although there is debate concerning the optimal conditions under which a stereotype is most likely to serve as the basis for judgment, it has been shown that stereotype consistent impressions occur when cognitive resources are taxed and the amount of information available is high (Macrae, Hewstone, & Griffiths, 1993). Capital jurors are inundated with large quantities of subjective information, and are provided with little guidance on how to use the material to reach a sentencing decision. As a result, the processing demands in a capital trial are high, and the task complex.

Jurors enter the sentencing phase with a defendant schema developed from their pre-existing stereotypes, the evidence presented during the guilt and deliberations phase of the trial, and possibly from external sources (e.g., pretrial publicity). The activated stereotypes associated with the defendant are likely to be integrated into this schema, affecting the subsequent defendant attribution hypothesis, when murder is perceived to be consistent with the stereotype expectations. Research has shown that stereotype expectations bias information processing in a confirmatory manner (see Hamilton & Sherman, 1994). Thus, once an attribution hypothesis has been formed, a biased information search is likely to ensue that focuses attention toward argument and evidence that is perceived to support the hypothesis and associated sentence. As a result of this biased search, jurors' schema-based defendant attributions are not likely to be rejected.

Bodenhausen and Wyer (1985) examined how perceivers evaluate diagnostic and non-diagnostic information that either supported or contradicted a given attribution. Three different types of information were included in the offender's case file: non-diagnostic background information (demographic characteristics), decision-relevant information (had implications for whether the target should be paroled), and life circumstances information (described the target's circumstances at or before the time of the crime). The use of this information was found to vary as a function of the activation of the stereotype and the resulting attribution. The offender's life circumstances that had implications for why the crime occurred were used as an explanation for the crime, resulting in greater leniency when no stereotype was activated. However, this information had no effect on parole recommendations when a stereotype was activated. Under these circumstances, participants based their sentence recommendations on the consistency between the crime and the associated stereotype (Bodenhausen & Wyer, 1985, p. 276).

Stereotype activation was also found to affect participants' ability to recall information that was either consistent or inconsistent with their attribution hypotheses. When a stereotype was not activated and when the life-circumstances information had implications for why the crime occurred, all three types of information were recalled better. Under these conditions, this information appeared to be used as a basis for making a defendant attribution, and as a result was integrated into the defendant schema. However, when a stereotype was activated, it served as a basis for the defendant attribution. When the crime was inconsistent with the stereotype, the ensuing attribution implied a situational cause. This resulted in a weak parole decision. Life circumstances information was integrated into the schema and recalled better when it also implied leniency (consistent with the stereotype). However, when the stereotype was activated, and the crime was consistent with it, the attribution led to an internal cause. Under these conditions, life circumstances information that implied leniency (inconsistent with the attribution) was not integrated into the defendant schema. The perceiver then focused on non-diagnostic subjective material (i.e., offender's background information). This subjective material was recalled better than the diagnostic life-circumstances information, suggesting that it was perceived to support the attribution.

These findings suggest that the activation of a stereotype results in an attribution hypothesis on the basis of the stereotype. A biased search then ensues in an effort to confirm this hypothesis. Confirmatory evidence is more likely than incongruous information to be integrated into the defendant schema. Thus, the initial attribution hypothesis is not likely to be refuted. Although these data offer insight into how congruous arguments are evaluated, they do not explain how arguments and information that are inconsistent with the attribution are processed.

The impact and evaluation of disconfirmatory material varies as a function of the situation. Hastie and Kumar (1979) found recall to be superior for material that was incongruous rather than congruous with a person impression. This finding is inconsistent with Bodenhausen and Wyer's (1985) results. According to Macrae et al. (1993), perceivers tend to show preferential recall for stereotype-inconsistent information when processing demands are low. However, stereotype expectations are likely to be confirmed when information is ambiguous or consistent with the accompanying stereotype expectations (Brewer, 1996, p. 237). As mentioned above, the capital trial is likely to tax cognitive resources. In addition, much of the evidence is ambiguous. As a result, mitigating evidence, e.g., drug abuse, may be misconstrued to support a negative attribution and an accompanying death sentence (see Lynch & Haney, 2000). Thus, the capital trial is likely to produce conditions where jurors favor consistent, not stereotype-inconsistent, evidence.

The penalty phase of a capital trial is a confrontational setting where jurors are bombarded with argument from both the defense and prosecution in an effort to persuade them to support a particular punishment position. This setting can be framed as a persuasion task. Research on selectivity in judgment has shown that perceivers are more critical of information that counters rather than confirms an attitude (Eagly & Chaiken, 1993, p. 596). Jurors may conduct a biased evaluation of argument that does not support their defendant attributions and pre-deliberation sentence positions. This is in line with the results reported by Bodenhausen and Wyer (1985). Participants had better recall for material that supported their sentence positions.

The theory of disconfirmation bias put forward by Edwards and Smith (1996) postulates that the presentation of an argument will activate material from memory relevant to the argument. When the argument is incompatible with prior beliefs, there is a bias to judge the argument as weak. The perceiver will engage in a deliberate memory search in an attempt to retrieve material that can be used to refute it.

Edwards and Smith tested their central thesis that "there is a bias to disconfirm arguments incompatible with one's position" (Edwards & Smith, 1996). Strength of prior beliefs on seven issues was measured, and participants who indicated an interest in participating in future studies were contacted four to six weeks later. This time delay is important in that a capital trial often spans over a period of several weeks. In addition, the sentencing phase presentation may take several days or longer to complete. If jurors' sentencing positions soften over time, then early race-based attributions may not have an effect on sentence outcomes. Phase two participants were presented with two arguments (one from each side) and then rated the strength of each argument. A questionnaire (filler task) was administered which was followed by a thought listing task where participants were presented with one of the arguments they had just evaluated and asked to write down as many thoughts as came to mind.

Individuals judged an argument that was incompatible with their prior beliefs as weak, spent more time scrutinizing the argument, generated a greater number of relevant thoughts and arguments in the thought-listing task, and produced a greater number of refutational than supportive arguments. These findings held for participants with strong and moderate views, regardless of prior belief position, and across time. A second experiment found bias to be accentuated when prior beliefs were associated with emotional conviction, a situation that often occurs within the capital trial context.

Jurors are likely to integrate sentence phase evidence and argument into their defendant schema that supports their defendant attribution, and make a cognitive effort to refute or minimize the relevance of evidence that is inconsistent with their pre-deliberation sentence position. In their experiment on sentencing and instruction comprehension, Lynch and Haney (2000) also looked at the effects of race on the evaluation of evidence. Not only was the offender's race found to have an effect on sentence outcomes, but it also influenced the way participants reacted and used mitigating information. Information on substance abuse, psychiatric problems and childhood abuse was regarded as significantly less mitigating in the black offender conditions than in the white offender conditions (Lynch & Haney, 2000, p. 352). These race effects were significant after controlling for instruction comprehension. Ambiguous information tends to be perceived to confirm a stereotype (Bodenhausen, & Macrae, 1996). Mitigating evidence, which is often subjective in meaning with regard to the implications of the crime (e.g., psychiatric impairment), was more likely to be interpreted to support a negative internal attribution and death sentence when the defendant was black. This finding suggests that participants discarded evidence that was incongruous with their defendant attributions and integrated information that was perceived to support their attributions.

Overall, the experimental literature suggests that a defendant attribution process is likely to occur during the sentencing phase of a capital trial that can be affected by the race of the defendant, when a racial stereotype is activated. These race-based attribution processes can in turn result in a biased evaluation of the evidence. In addition, the effect of the defendant's race on final sentence outcomes is likely to be moderated by variables that inhibit heuristic processing or enhance the salience of white jurors' egalitarian values.

LIMITATIONS TO THE EXPERIMENTAL RESEARCH

Several legitimate criticisms have been raised concerning the internal and external validity of the "mock jury" research, and as a result, its utility has been called into question. Some of these criticisms stem from these studies' inability to capture the important external properties of a capital trial. Such qualities include:

> The characteristics of the jurors, the physical setting, the medium used to present evidence and arguments, the realism of voir dire and death qualification, the size of the jury, the

> length of deliberations, the realism of the voting procedure, and the nature of the decision required (Costanzo & Costanzo, 1992, p.191).

More importantly, these studies do not capture the inherent cognitive and affective nature of the courtroom phenomena. The ultimate consequences of a sentence decision, the emotional nature of a murder, the pressures on jurors, and the complexity of the sentencing task are just some of the important components of a capital trial that the experimental studies cannot and often do not attempt to capture. In the words of one juror, "it was traumatic. It was terrible, and I'm still shaken. I just hope I never have to go through something like that again" (Hans, 1988 p. 170). As a result, the process these researchers are studying may be very different from the process that real jurors go through when evaluating evidence and reaching sentencing decisions.

Stereotypes are most likely to have an impact on decisions when information-processing demands are complex (Bodenhausen & Wyer, 1985). The low to moderate levels of cognitive demand in many of the experiments on sentencing may have attenuated the impact that race had on participants' decisions. It is reasonable to postulate that the means by which the race of the defendant affects the cognitive evaluation process in study participants may also impact jurors' sentencing decisions. The magnitude of this effect may even be more pronounced in the capital trial setting where cognitive capacity is taxed, evidence is complex, and task ambiguity high, than in the contrived environment of the laboratory.

CHAPTER 5

DEVELOPING A MODEL OF JUROR AND JURY DECISION-MAKING

WHAT IS IMPORTANT: RACE-OF-OFFENDER VS. RACE-OF-VICTIM

As discussed in the previous chapter, the experimental research on sentencing tends to contradict the archival literature. According to the archival findings, the race of the victim has a significant impact on jury sentencing outcomes. A significant race-of-defendant effect has not been found consistently or as a main effect. With respect to the experimental literature, the offender's race has a significant effect on participants' sentencing decisions (See Kan & Phillips, 2003). However, the race of the victim does not appear typically to be important. This discrepancy is difficult to reconcile.

Because the archival literature uses actual jury outcomes, its external validity is not in question. This cannot be said for the experimental studies on race and sentencing. The stimulus materials provided by experimenters typically provide brief written summaries, which often focus the participants' attention towards the defendant, not the victim. However, the liberty provided by the Supreme Court to the state in reference to the use of victim impact evidence is likely to shift jurors' attention towards the victim. A juror interviewed by the Capital Jury Project reported an instance where the:

> Prosecutor staged a dramatic reenactment of the crime, how the victims were, how they were shot. He got on his knees in dramatic fashion and he started crying and talked about how the guy had two seconds to live and what do 'you' think if you only had two seconds to live and 'you' had a gun pointed to the back of your head (Bowers et al., 2001, p. 247).

The emotional quality of the evidence presented in a capital trial is also lacking in the experimental material. One researcher described the capital juror experience as follows:

> ...They look at pictures of murdered victims; watch patiently as surviving family members cry on the witness stand; and hear the grim, frightening details of crimes that seem to defy explanation... confront another layer of tragedy and horror; the painful life story of the defendant; himself often the victim of shocking mistreatment, abuse and neglect (Haney, Sontag, & Costanzo, 1994, p.150).

The conflicting findings between the archival and experimental literature may be attributed to the quality of the stimulus materials in the typical experimental study. Sweeney and Haney (1992) conducted a meta-analysis on race-of-defendant effects in the experimental literature. Studies that demonstrated greater methodological rigor—photographic images, specified racial composition of subject sample, and the control of the victim's race—consistently uncovered racial bias in sentencing decisions. The correlation between effect size and the "medium," whether or not the race of the defendant was communicated via written words or pictorially, was .42. Like the race-of-defendant effects found by Sweeney and Haney (1992), the heterogeneity of the race-of-victim effects found in the meta-analysis conducted by Mazzella and Feingold (1994) may be attributed to variation in methodological rigor. When victim manipulation is poor and simplistic, the likelihood that participants will display empathy towards the victim is low. The experimental studies may be failing to manufacture the context in which victim-race effects are most likely to occur. Perhaps if researchers provided emotional stimulus materials that focused participants' attention towards the victim, victim effects would be more pronounced. This is precisely what was found in one of the few studies that did so.

Greene, Koehring and Quiat, (1998) looked at the effects of victim impact statements on participants' assessments of the victim, the survivors, the offense, mitigating and aggravating evidence, and the defendant. Participants who answered an ad were asked if they were registered to vote or had a driver's license. Those that answered, "yes" to one of these questions watched one of two abridged versions of the *Booth* trial where the respectability of the victim was manipulated in the victim impact statement.

Although participants were not asked to reach a sentence decision, the highly respectable victims were evaluated more positively than the less respectable victims on all three dimensions—likableness, decency, and value. More importantly, the murders of the respectable victims were rated as more serious than the murders of the less respectable victims. This suggests that when researchers direct participants' attention toward the victim with a quality victim manipulation, victim effects do appear.

With respect to the archival method, the nature of the data often precludes an examination into how jurors evaluate the types of evidence a defendant provides as an excuse or justification for his or her behavior, or the effect race has on this evaluation process. As a result, this method may tend to overlook the effects that the race-of-defendant variable has on sentencing.

Because both bodies of literature are insufficient on important pieces of the puzzle, it is likely that both the race of the victim and defendant have an effect on sentencing. The post-trial interview literature supports such a hypothesis. A comprehensive model on sentencing should be consistent with the archival data, account for the discrepancies between the experimental and archival literature, and provide an explanation for how and when race affects sentence outcomes.

PUTTING IT ALL TOGETHER

Findings from the experimental and archival literature suggest that the effects of the defendant and victim race may be independent from one another, in support of a dual process model. Lynch and Haney (2000) did not find any main race-of-victim effects. However, the race-of-defendant had a significant impact on the evaluation of mitigating information. In addition, Greene et al. (1998) found that the ratings of the defendant and aggravating circumstances were not influenced by the victim variable. Finally, in their study on race and sentencing in Philadelphia, Baldus et al. (1998) found that the race of the victim did not have an effect on the weight jurors gave to mitigating evidence; however, the race of the defendant did affect jurors' mitigating evidence evaluations. Thus, the proposed dual process model predicts that jurors undergo two independent processes when reaching a sentence position before deliberations begin—victim evaluations and defendant attributions. The race of the victim and defendant are hypothesized to influence pre-deliberation sentence positions through their impact on these two processes.

For purposes of the research undertaken here, the dual process model of sentencing is developed most fully with respect to white jurors in capital cases confronted with black defendants and either white or black victims. The reason for this is the nature of the data: insufficient numbers of black jurors are included in the samples of the Capital Jury Project to test the model of victim evaluation and defendant attribution as applied to them. An extension of the model to black jurors could be made straightforwardly with the same reasoning based on social categorization, social comparison, in-group identification, victim evaluation, and defendant attribution. In addition, this research is limited to cases with black defendants. This is also a result of the data provided by the Capital Jury Project. Only black-defendant/white-victim and black-defendant/-black victim cases were included in the dataset. Race-of-defendant effects to be observed require variation within the race of defendant variable. This limited the examination of the defendant attribution process.

It is important to note that the proposed model is limited to jurors' pre-deliberation sentence positions. The relationship between juror sentence positions and jury sentence decisions is likely to be influenced by the deliberations process. As a result, a model of jury sentencing must take this into account. The proposed model can be extended to account for deliberations and jury sentencing. The clarity of the normative structure governing the sentencing task and the salience of jurors' egalitarian values is hypothesized to moderate the relationship between juror pre-deliberation sentence positions and jury sentence outcomes. These factors are predicted to come into play once the deliberations begin. The proposed dual process model of juror sentencing positions and its extension to final sentence outcomes are developed below.

The Victim Evaluation Process

Decisions such as *Payne v. Tennessee* increase the prominence of the victim in the sentencing phase in a capital trial by the introduction of victim-impact statements. Victim evaluations are likely to have an effect on the perceived severity of the crime (see Greene et al., 1998; Greene, 1999). The race of the victim may have an influence on sentence positions through its impact on victim evaluations. Jurors should display more empathy and positive affect towards victims and their families who are of the same race as the juror. Research has found strong support for an in-group bias effect (see Mullen, Brown, & Smith, 1992). Thus, victim evaluations may be affected by race when the victim is categorized as a member of a particular racial group.

The Psychological Process of In-group Identification and Out-group Derogation

According to social identity theory, prejudice begins with the categorization of social objects into groups, or social categorizations. These categorizations divide the social world into distinct categories, provide individuals with a point of self-reference, and define members as similar to or different from members of other relevant groups (Turner, 1982, p. 17).

The salience of a given category affects the likelihood that it will serve as a basis for categorization (Hamilton & Trolier, 1986). African Americans are underrepresented in the jury, the judiciary, and in the district attorney's office.[13] Thus, an African American defendant is quite distinct. As a result, race is likely to be a salient category in the courtroom setting. When race is salient, the juror will categorize himself and other social objects, including the defendant and victim, into their respective racial groups. Members of the same racial group as the juror are categorized as in-group members and those of a different racial group as out-group members. This is known as the *social comparison process* (Stets & Burke, 2000, p. 225). Thus, in black-defendant/white-victim homicide, white jurors will categorize the victim as an in-group member and the defendant as an out-group member. White jurors in black-defendant/black-victim homicides will categorize both the defendant and victim as out-group members.

The social comparison process can have an effect on how in-group and out-group members are evaluated under certain circumstances. According to Taijfel's *categorization law*, members of a given group are assigned all of the characteristics perceived to be stereotypical of their category when social category membership is made salient (Turner, 1982, p. 28). As a result, there will be a tendency to exaggerate the differences on important attributes and characteristics between members of disparate groups and minimize these differences within groups. Group membership salience also cultivates perceived intra-group similarity and intra-group liking (Turner, 1982, pp. 28-29). Thus, the perceived differences between the self and members of the out-group, and the perceived similarities between the self and members of the in-group, will be accentuated for all the attitudes, beliefs, attributes, and other properties believed to be correlated with the relevant social category.

In accordance with Taijfel's categorization law, when race serves as the basis for social comparison and group membership is salient, jurors will tend to perceive a victim who is a member of the in-group to

---

[13] Dieter (1998) reported that only one percent of the district attorneys in death penalty states were black. The Judicial Selection Project reported in their annual report that blacks made up only 10% of the Federal Judiciary in 1998 (See Judicial selection project: annual report, 1998. http://www.afj.org/98anl1.html accessed 11/11/99). This discrepancy carries over into the state and county judiciary, which is often made up of former prosecutors and attorneys.

be similar to themselves on self-relevant dimensions and victims who are categorized as out-group members as dissimilar. Research on in-group and out-group evaluations has shown that people tend to evaluate members of the in-group more positively than members of the out-group, when group membership is salient.

Sachdev and Bourhis (1991) manipulated status, power, and group size in a minimal group paradigm study. Responses to a questionnaire indicated that participants liked in-group members more than out-group members, and felt that other in-group members liked them. In addition, in-group/out-group categorization was sufficient to produce this in-group bias effect. A meta-analysis incorporating 37 studies on in-group bias conducted by Mullen et al. (1992) also concluded that the in-group is evaluated more positively than the out-group.

The in-group bias effect is likely to have an influence on jurors' victim evaluations when the victim is categorized as a member of the in-group. Jurors are more likely to empathize with victims and their families when they are perceived to be similar to themselves on important self-relevant dimensions. Race effects on victim evaluations should be strongest when group membership is made salient, the victim is categorized as a member of the in-group, and jurors' identification with the in-group is high (Mullen et al., 1992). In-group identification is at its peak when behavior and evaluations are made on the basis of group membership (Taijfel & Turner, 1986). Although researchers do not agree on whether in-group identification is sufficient to elicit in-group bias, they do agree that it is a necessary prerequisite for discrimination (Leonardelli & Brewer, 2001, p. 470). Several factors including group salience have an impact on in-group identification.

Mullen et al. (1992) found that group salience was most often manipulated by varying in-group size and the realness of the group. There are several factors in the courtroom that should enhance group salience. One of these variables includes perceived conflict. Research has shown that intergroup conflict enhances group salience and perceived similarity with other in-group members (see Holtz & Miller, 1985). Thus, group salience and in-group identification should be high in interracial homicide, where intergroup tension is at its peak.

Group membership may also affect white jurors' victim evaluations in intra-racial homicide, where both the defendant and victim are members of the out-group. Research has shown that the novelty and unusualness of a stimulus can enhance group salience (see Hamilton, 1981). White jurors may have infrequent encounters with African Americans. In addition, undesirable behaviors, i.e., capital murder, are also novel in that they occur with relative infrequency (Hamilton, & Trolier, 1986, pp. 135-136). The co-occurrence of an encounter with an African American defendant charged with capital murder should enhance the salience of the out-group for white jurors. Activation of the out-group has been shown to activate the corresponding in-group category (see Wilder & Shapiro, 1984). Thus, group membership may also be salient for white jurors in black-defendant/black-victim trials. Under these circumstances, the novelty of the situation may also result in a social categorization and social comparison process on the premise of race. White jurors will categorize both the victim and the defendant as members of the out-group. The activation of the out-group will then activate the corresponding in-group.

Interviews by the Capital Jury Project of whites who served as jurors in black-defendant/black-victim homicide provides some anecdotal evidence of a social categorization, social comparison, and in-group identification process on the basis of race, resulting in the tendency to perceive differences between in-group and out-group members (emphasis added):

> I didn't know who *they* [the victims] were, but I was impressed from the trial that there are *two definite lifestyles.* The *black community* was entirely *different* from the way I was raised and the way *we* lived. The value of life—it's totally *different* (Vandiver, 1997).

Another juror stated:

> ...when I heard about the killing, I thought, well, *they're* just wiping each other out again. You know, if *they'd* been white people, I would've had a *different attitude.* I'm sorry that I feel that way (Vandiver, 1997).

In-group bias has been shown to be associated with enhanced in-group evaluation, not out-group derogation (see Brewer & Campbell,

1976; Rabbie & Horwitz, 1969; Ryen & Kahn, 1975). Therefore, categorization of the victim as a member of the out-group is not likely to result in open hostility toward the victim. However, the social comparison and in-group identification process are likely to influence jurors' victim evaluations within these contexts. Pettigrew and Meertens' (1995) research on seven Western European nations found support for a subtle form of prejudice against out-group members. This form of prejudice is associated with low negative emotions and the absence of positive feelings. Thus, in-group bias may manifest itself as the withholding of positive affect and empathy toward victims and their families when they are categorized as members of the out-group. This withholding of positive affect and empathy is likely to results in low victim evaluations.

Victim Evaluation and Sentencing

According to the victim evaluation component of the dual process model, the murder of a positively evaluated victim is perceived to be more severe than the murder of a less positively evaluated victim. The impact of race on this evaluation is contingent upon jurors' tendencies to categorize the victim as an in-group or out-group member on the premise of race. Race is likely to serve as the basis for victim categorization when it is a salient feature in the capital trial setting. Jurors will perceive themselves to be similar to the victim on self-relevant attributes when the victim is categorized as an in-group member, the social comparison process occurs, and in-group identification is high. Perceived similarity should cultivate positive affect and empathy. This positive affect, and the ability to take the perspective of the victim and his or her family, should have a positive influence on victim evaluations.

Victims categorized as members of the out-group activate the corresponding in-group when group membership is salient. Jurors will perceive themselves to be different from the victim and his or her corresponding group on self-relevant attributes. Perceived dissimilarity should lead to the withholding of positive affect and empathy toward the victim and his or her family, which will have a negative influence on victim evaluations.

The effects of in-group bias on white jurors' victim evaluations should be strongest in interracial homicides, where the defendant is black and the victim is white, and group tension is at its peak. Under these conditions, the processes of group categorization and social comparison on the premise of race are most likely to occur. The effects of race on white jurors' victim evaluations should be insignificant in white-defendant/white-victim homicides, where the salience of racial social categories is low. As a result, race-based social comparison and in-group identification are unlikely to occur.

The probability of a pre-deliberation death sentence position is expected to increase linearly as a function of positive victim evaluations. Accordingly, white jurors will be more likely to favor a death sentence when the victim is white than when he is black. The reciprocal should occur for black jurors. However, there are several factors that serve to reduce the odds that a black juror will sit on a capital trial (e.g., death qualification, small numbers in jury pool, use of peremptory challenges). Thus, it is unlikely that black in-group bias will counteract the effects of white in-group bias. Figure 1 illustrates the victim evaluation process.

Evaluation of the Defendant

The categorization process should also have an effect on jurors' defendant evaluations when group membership is salient. Under these conditions, white jurors will categorize a defendant in a black-defendant/white-victim or black-defendant/black-victim homicide into the out-group. This should lead to the withholding of positive affect and empathy toward the defendant. As a result, white jurors will be unlikely to display compassion or mercy toward the defendant. Bowers et al. (2001) reported that only 4 percent of white jurors in the interracial homicide condition indicated that the defendant deserved mercy because he was sorry.

Black jurors may empathize with a black defendant when the social comparison process occurs, resulting in compassion and mercy toward the defendant. However, consistent with the 'black sheep' effect (see Marques, Yzerbyt, & Leyens, 1988), they may also try to distance themselves from African American defendants who commit actions which diminish the status of the group, resulting in a greater degree of punitiveness (Rector & Bagby, 1997). Approximately 32 percent of black jurors in the interracial condition reported that the defendant deserved mercy because he was sorry, in contrast to only 6 percent in the black-defendant/black-victim condition (Bowers et al., 2001, p. 214). Thus, black jurors do appear to feel more mercy for black defendants in conditions where race-based social categorization, social comparison, and in-group identification are most likely to occur. Consequently, group categorization of the defendant should affect significantly sentence preferences.

The Defendant Attribution Process

Stereotypes are most likely to have an impact on decisions when information-processing demands are complex (Bodenhausen & Wyer, 1985). The quantity and ambiguity of sentencing phase evidence, coupled with the novelty, complexity and poor instructional guidance provided by the court is likely to tax processing resources. When jurors resort to their own devices, they may revert to heuristic processing techniques that have served them well in the past to make an attribution for the cause of the defendant's behavior. Stereotypes and pre-existing defendant schemas developed throughout the course of the trial are likely to have an effect on jurors' attributions and evidence evaluations.

When jurors resort to heuristic processing, and the crime is consistent with the activated race-based stereotype, a negative internal attribution is likely to ensue. Thus, violent crime must be perceived by jurors to be a stereotypical attribute of African Americans before an internal attribution is likely to be made. Results from survey research suggest that violence is associated with African Americans. Chiricos et al. (2004) reported that respondents overestimated black involvement in violent crime. Furthermore, approximately 37 percent of the sample surveyed in a Gallup Poll conducted in December 1993, perceived blacks as "more likely" than other groups to commit crimes. The homeless were the only group that was evaluated to be more criminally inclined than blacks. It is possible that discrepancies would be even greater if African Americans were not included in the sample or if a more subtle question was posed to measure prejudice.

Race-based stereotypes are often developed and passed down through a sociocultural process. The institutions of socialization, particularly the mass media, often foment the association between race and crime. . Johnson (1987) studied the images of blacks portrayed in the local media in Boston. Johnson found that 85 percent of the stories

Figure 1: The victim evaluation process of the dual process model

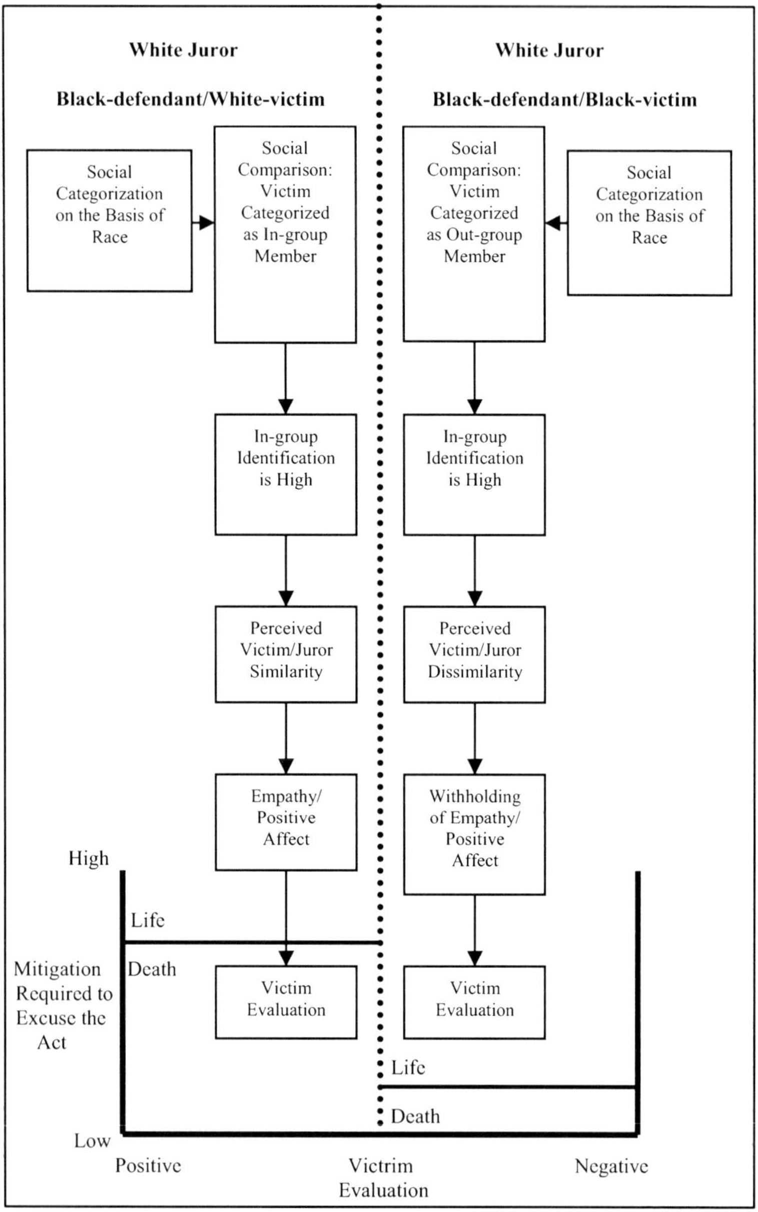

White Juror

Black-defendant/White-victim

Social Categorization on the Basis of Race

Social Comparison: Victim Categorized as In-group Member

In-group Identification is High

Perceived Victim/Juror Similarity

Empathy/ Positive Affect

Victim Evaluation

White Juror

Black-defendant/Black-victim

Social Comparison: Victim Categorized as Out-group Member

Social Categorization on the Basis of Race

In-group Identification is High

Perceived Victim/Juror Dissimilarity

Withholding of Empathy/ Positive Affect

Victim Evaluation

High

Life

Death

Mitigation Required to Excuse the Act

Life

Death

Low

Positive

Victrim Evaluation

Negative

about the two predominately black neighborhoods in Boston focused on crime or violent accidents, portraying African Americans as victims or perpetrators of violence (Johnson, 1987, p. 50). Although the two neighborhoods accounted for only 7 percent of the total crime news, 59 percent of all the news items about the two neighborhoods were about crime. Johnson succinctly summarized the negative coverage and the effects of this bias as follows:

> The major-media news about Boston's predominately black neighborhoods is biased in the direction of commonly held stereotypes about blacks and the poor... a typical news consumer might easily come to associate the prevailing negative images with all inner-city blacks (Johnson, 1987, pp. 50-51).

The mass media's biased coverage of African American neighborhoods perpetuates the image of a community wracked by crime and violence. As a result, it is likely that an "African American" stereotype that associates race with violent crime is widespread. Thus, when heuristic processing occurs, murder may be perceived by some to be more stereotypical behavior for African American defendants, in support of a negative internal attribution.

Once an attribution has been made, jurors will conduct a biased search in an attempt to confirm their schema-based hypothesis (see Darley & Gross, 1983). Evidence and argument that is perceived to be consistent with the defendant schema and attribution hypothesis will be integrated into the defendant schema. Jurors will make a cognitive effort to disconfirm evidence and argument that is inconsistent with their defendant schema, attribution, and the corresponding sentence. This is consistent with Lynch and Haney's (2000) results, which indicated that when a race-based internal attribution supported a death sentence (i.e., black defendant), jurors tended to reject mitigating evidence that was inconsistent with the attribution, and perceive ambiguous mitigating evidence—substance abuse, psychiatric problems, and a history of child abuse—to support their positions

Defendant Attributions and Sentencing

As illustrated in Figure 2, negative internal attribution tends to support a death sentence. An external and some internal attributions (e.g., behavior attributed to the youth of the defendant) support a life sentence. A negative internal attribution is likely to ensue when white jurors' defendant schemas are associated with a race-based stereotype, and the murder conviction is consistent with that stereotype. As a result, the excuses and justifications provided by the defendant, and the evidence proffered by the state, will be either refuted or accepted and integrated into jurors' defendant schemas on the basis of whether it is perceived to support or conflict with the attribution hypothesis.

When mitigating evidence is inconsistent with a negative internal attribution, it is less likely to influence pre-deliberation sentence positions. Aggravating and ambiguous mitigating evidence that is perceived to support jurors' negative internal attributions will be given more weight and integrated into their sentencing position. This biased evaluation process is likely to result in the confirmation of the negative internal attribution inferred from the stereotype, and the rejection of the external or internal attribution asserted by the defendant.

The Effect of the Egalitarian Value System on Final Sentence Outcomes: Some Moderators

Whether or not the effects of race on pre-deliberation sentence positions will carry over and influence the jury's final sentence outcome is predicted to be moderated by the clarity of the normative structure that governs the sentencing task and the salience of jurors' egalitarian values. These factors come into play once deliberations begin.

Normative Structure

According to the aversive racism perspective as conceptualized by Gaertner and Dovidio (1986), aversive racists are strongly motivated to avoid acting in recognizably inappropriate ways in interracial contexts. Racial discrimination is most likely to occur when the normative structure within the situation is "weak, ambiguous, or conflicting," or when the behavior can be attributed to factors other than race (Gaertner & Dovidio, 1986, p. 66).

Figure 2: The defendant attribution process of the dual process model

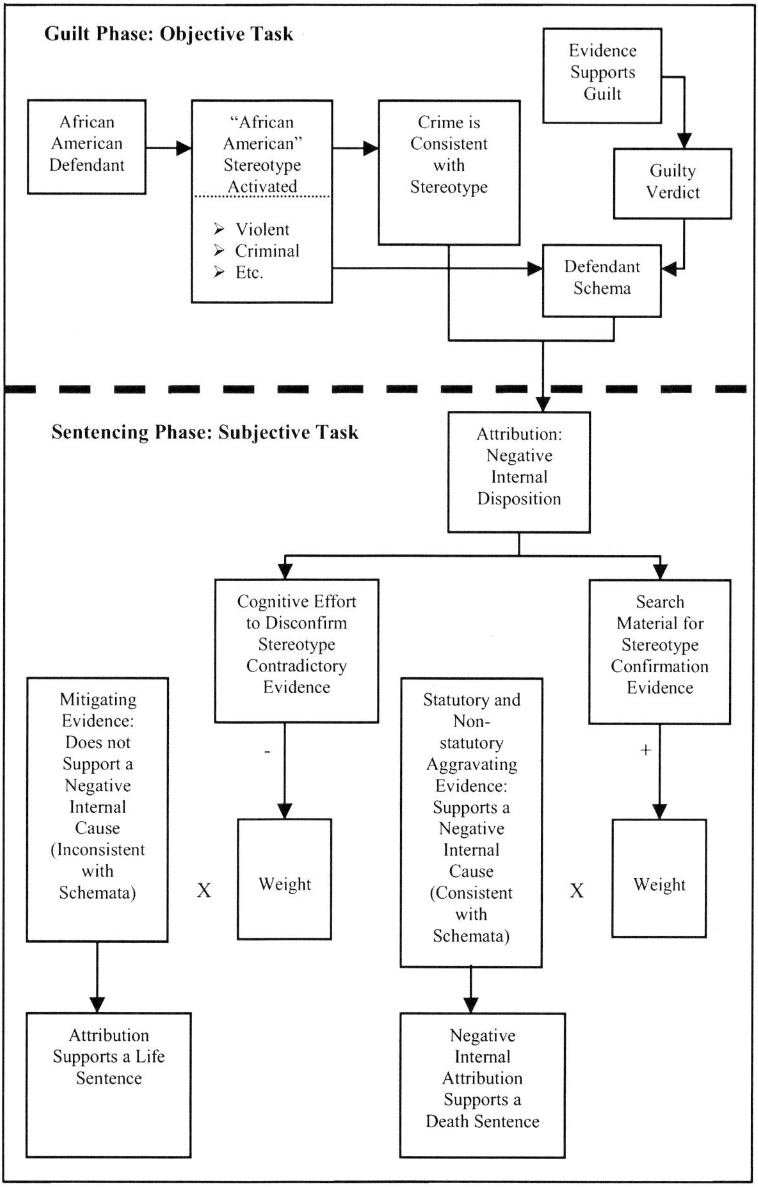

Guilt Phase: Objective Task

Evidence Supports Guilt

African American Defendant

"African American" Stereotype Activated

- Violent
- Criminal
- Etc.

Crime is Consistent with Stereotype

Guilty Verdict

Defendant Schema

Sentencing Phase: Subjective Task

Attribution: Negative Internal Disposition

Cognitive Effort to Disconfirm Stereotype Contradictory Evidence

Search Material for Stereotype Confirmation Evidence

-

\+

Mitigating Evidence: Does not Support a Negative Internal Cause (Inconsistent with Schemata)

X

Weight

Statutory and Non-statutory Aggravating Evidence: Supports a Negative Internal Cause (Consistent with Schemata)

X

Weight

Attribution Supports a Life Sentence

Negative Internal Attribution Supports a Death Sentence

When situations are unambiguous, and prejudice cannot be rationalized, racial discrimination is unlikely to occur.

Due to the novelty of the capital trial, jurors are not likely to hold a specific pre-existing normative structure governing behavior in the courtroom. As a result, the normative structure is likely socially constructed over the course of the trial through the instructions provided by the judge and attorneys, and the interactions between the jurors. If this process fails to construct a clear normative structure that provides sufficient guidance, disavows the use of race, or provides white jurors with nonracial features that can be used to justify discriminatory sentencing, then race is more likely to affect sentence outcomes.

Evidence ambiguity, jury composition, instruction comprehension, and instruction guidance are four factors that may have an impact on the development of the normative structure in a capital trial, the perceived presence or absence of non-racial justifications for discriminatory sentencing, and the likelihood that white jurors will activate their egalitarian values. Stereotypes are unlikely to manifest themselves in final sentencing decisions when a clear normative structure is developed that constrains race-based decision heuristics (i.e., instruction comprehension is high); evidence is strong in one direction or the other (i.e., either strongly supports a life or death sentence); racial tension and jurors' egalitarian ideals are made salient (i.e., a black male is on the jury); and race-based sentencing cannot be rationalized (i.e., jury instructions provide detailed guidelines for evaluating evidence and reaching a decision). Stereotypes are most likely to have an impact on decisions when instruction comprehension is low, the jury is all white, jurors are "liberated" by the evidence, and race-based sentencing can be rationalized (i.e., the instructions do not provide much guidance). Under these conditions, the normative structure is weak, and white jurors' egalitarian ideals are less likely to suppress the effects of stereotypes on their pre-deliberation sentence positions. As a result, pre-deliberation sentence positions are likely to carry over into the final sentence outcome.

TESTING THE MODEL: HYPOTHESES AND PREDICTIONS

This study will test the predictions made by the dual process model and the effects of race on defendant attribution, victim evaluations, and pre-deliberation sentence positions and outcomes.

Hypothesis 1: The race of the victim affects white jurors' empathy toward the victim.

Prediction 1a: White jurors display more empathy toward the victim and his family in interracial (black-defendant/white-victim) as compared to intra-racial (black-defendant/black-victim) homicide.

Interracial homicide (black-defendant/white-victim) cases may differ significantly from intra-racial homicide (black-defendant/black-victim) cases on factors that could be associated with empathy. If so, these factors, not race, may explain the relationship between empathy and racial category. However, it is believed that race is related to empathy after taking these potential confounds into account.

> *Prediction 1ai: The relationship between empathy and race is significant after controlling for the gender of the victim*
>
> *Prediction 1aii: The relationship between empathy and race is significant after controlling for the marital status of the victim.*
>
> *Prediction 1aiii: The relationship between empathy and race is significant after controlling for the socioeconomic status of the juror.*
>
> *Prediction 1aiv: The relationship between empathy and race is significant after controlling for whether or not the victim had children.*

Hypothesis 2: Empathy toward the victim and his family affects white jurors' victim evaluations.

Prediction 2a: White jurors' victim evaluations are more positive when empathy toward the victim and his family is high.

Prediction 2b: White jurors' victim evaluations are more positive in interracial (black-defendant/white-victim) as compared to intra-racial (black-defendant/black-victim) homicide.

Prediction 2bi: The relationship between victim evaluations and race is significant after controlling for the deathworthiness score.

Prediction 2bii: The relationship between victim evaluations and race is significant after controlling for the gender of the victim

Prediction 2biii: The relationship between victim evaluations and race is significant after controlling for whether or not the victim had children.

Prediction 2biv: The relationship between victim evaluations and race is significant after controlling for the marital status of the victim.

Prediction 2bv: The relationship between victim evaluations and race is significant after controlling for the socioeconomic status of the juror.

Hypothesis 3: The murder of a positively evaluated victim is more likely to result in support for a death sentence than the murder of a less positively evaluated victim.

Prediction 3a: There is a positive relationship between favorability of victim evaluations and the probability that white jurors' pre-deliberation sentence positions will favor death.

Hypothesis 4: The perceived dangerousness of a black defendant is affected by the race of the juror.

Prediction 4a: White jurors are more likely than black jurors to describe a black defendant as dangerous to other people.

Hypothesis 5: White jurors perceptions of the danger posed by black defendants affects their evaluation of mitigating evidence.

Prediction 5a: White jurors who describe the black defendant as dangerous to other people, are more likely than those who do not, to believe that the evidence proves that he would be dangerous in the future.

Prediction 5b: White jurors who describe the black defendant as dangerous to other people give less weight to mitigating evidence than those who do not.

Hypothesis 6: The defendant attribution process is independent of the victim evaluation process.

Prediction 6a: The race of the victim is not significantly related to white jurors' perceptions of dangerousness.

Prediction 6b: White jurors' victim evaluations are not significantly related to their mitigating evidence evaluations.

The dual process model postulates that juror pre-deliberation sentence positions are the product of two independent processes, victim evaluations and defendant attributions. Jurors are expected to make an attribution judgment for the defendant's behavior, which will influence the weight jurors give to mitigating evidence. Jurors are also expected to make an evaluative judgment of the victim, which affects the perceived heinousness of the crime. Race is hypothesized to have an impact on sentencing via these two judgment processes. The race of the victim is predicted to influence jurors' victim evaluations, and the race of the defendant is predicted to influence defendant attributions.

Model Overall Path Analysis: According to the dual process model, the victim evaluation process mediates the effect of the race of the victim on white jurors' sentence positions. The defendant attribution process is predicted to bias the evaluation of mitigating evidence. Do white jurors reach their sentencing positions through the cognitive processes identified in the Dual Process Model?

The dual process model has also been extended to account for jury sentencing decisions. The strength of the evidence, jury composition, instruction comprehension, and instructional guidance are predicted to moderate the relationship between jurors' internally held sentence positions and the jury's final sentence decisions. These variables are predicted to either aid in the development of the normative structure that guides behavior in the sentencing task or to affect the salience of jurors' egalitarian values.

Model Extension to Final Sentence Outcomes: Consistent with the aversive racism perspective, the relationship between pre-deliberation sentence positions and sentence outcome (final sentence verdict) is likely to be moderated by the salience of white jurors' egalitarian values and the clarity of the sentencing task. When are pre-deliberation sentence positions likely to carry over into final sentence outcomes?

CHAPTER 6

RESEARCH DESIGN AND PROCEDURES

This study tested the hypotheses and research questions identified in the previous chapter, which required that all cases studied had black defendants. The Capital Jury Project (CJP) provided secondary data from face-to-face interviews conducted with over 1,100 capital jurors from 14 states. A detailed description of the data collection process is provided herein. These data encompassed 143 cases where the victim was either white or black, and the defendant was sentenced to life or death. These 143 cases were screened using the study's criteria—i.e., adequate recall of the punishment phase evidence and deliberations, and reported their race—which are described below. The final screened sample consisted of 139 cases and 367 jurors. Additional case specific data were collected from Lexis/Nexis published opinions. These data, coupled with juror case descriptions, were used to create a "deathworthiness" scale, so that cases could be classified together on the basis of crime, defendant, and victim(s) characteristics.

Two sampling techniques were used when the juror was the appropriate unit of analysis. The single juror method randomly selected a white juror from each case in the sample. The multi-juror method included every white juror within each case in the sample. Juror scores were aggregated within each case when the jury was the appropriate unit of analysis. Analyses and sample size varied depending on the particular hypothesis and its accompanying predictions. Various statistical analyses were used to create the conditions to test the hypotheses and complete those tests. These statistical procedures included factor analyses, hierarchical linear modeling (HLM), logistic regression, and other procedures.

PARTICIPANTS IN THE CAPITAL JURY PROJECT

A three-stage cluster sampling method was used to select jurors, which began at the state level. Multistage sampling can have a negative effect on the sample standard error when clusters are of unequal size. When this occurs, the elements within smaller clusters have a greater likelihood of being selected than elements in larger clusters. However, when clusters are of equal size, the estimation process is equivalent to simple random sampling, (Lee, Forthofer, & Lorimor, 1989, p. 12). All capital juries are made up of twelve jurors. Thus, there was not a need to adjust the standard error for bias resulting from the sampling design.

Sample Design

Stage 1 Sample: States

Eight states were chosen by the CJP that met the following study criteria: represents the principal variations in guided discretion statutes; sufficient volume of capital trials to meet the sampling quota for each state; and regional diversification. Data from the following states were included: California, Florida, Indiana, Kentucky, Pennsylvania, South Carolina, Texas, and Virginia. Four additional states were selected after the first year of the study to improve the representativeness of the sample: Georgia, Louisiana, North Carolina, and Tennessee. New Jersey and Alabama were brought into the study several years later (Bowers, 1995, p. 1078). These states represent capital punishment systems among Western, Southwestern, Midwestern, Mid-Atlantic, Border, and Southern states.

Stage 2 Sample: Capital Cases

A sample of capital trials from each state that made it through the guilt and sentencing phase was drawn from all such trials that took place after January 1988.[14] Sample quotas varied from 20 to 30 trials per state. Regardless of the quota size, each sample was partitioned so that half of the cases resulted in death sentences and the remaining half in life sentences.

Although the process by which cases were selected varied, the researchers attempted to choose recent cases in an effort to improve the reliability of jurors' recall. In some instances (e.g., Florida), random samples were drawn from the entire population of capital trials since 1988. In other instances, a random sample was drawn from the population of cases that resulted in life sentences, and a separate sample was drawn from the population of cases that resulted in death sentences. Due to financial and logistical limitations resulting from the sheer size of the state, sampling was restricted to cases within specified areas in California, Florida, and Texas (Bowers, 1995, p. 1080).

Stage 3 Sample: Jurors

A systematic sampling technique was developed in an attempt to interview four jurors from each trial. A strict sampling procedure was followed to ensure randomness and reduce the effects of selection bias. Each juror was allocated a number ranging from 1 to 12 corresponding to his or her order on the jury list. A starting point was then selected at random, and from that starting point, jurors were assigned sample status designations: A1, B1, C1; A2, B2, C2; A3, B3, C3; and A4, B4, C4. Panel A jurors represented the first wave of jurors. Up to five attempts were made throughout the day over a three-day period to arrange for an interview. If a Panel A juror refused to participate or could not be reached after three days, she or he was replaced with the corresponding Panel B juror. Five attempts were then made to schedule an interview with the Panel B juror. If this failed, the Panel A juror was replaced with the corresponding Panel C juror. If the Panel C juror could not be contacted or refused to participate, the next Panel B juror in the sequence was approached and so on (Bowers, 1995, p. 1081). This process continued until the sampling quota was met.

---

[14] Cases prior to 1988 were drawn in some cases to meet the quota.

The Sample: Selecting Capital Cases and Jurors

The initial sample provided by the Capital Jury Project encompassed 143 cases and 430 capital jurors. Eighty of the 143 cases involved black defendant(s) and white victim(s), and 63 included black defendant(s) and black victim(s). The number of jurors per case ranged from one to seven, and averaged 3.2.[15] Fifteen jurors were excluded because they either did not report their race, or reported a racial designation other than black or white. An additional 48 jurors were excluded because they reported that they either remembered the punishment phase evidence and/or sentencing deliberations "not so well" or "not at all." The cleaned sample encompassed of 139 cases—76 black-defendant/white-victim and 63 black-defendant/black-victim—and 367 jurors.

The Question of the Unit of Analysis: Threats to Statistical Conclusion Validity

Although the study hypotheses suggest that the juror (individual level) not the jury (group level) should be the unit of analysis, two factors had to be weighed before this decision could be made. First, most traditional multivariate statistics require that observations be independent from one another (Kashy & Kenny, 2000, p. 452). As is the case in most quasi-experimental designs, jurors were not randomly assigned to conditions, or prohibited from interacting with one another. Juror interactions (e.g., deliberations) are likely to have affected their perceptions of the evidence, the victim, the defendant, and final sentencing positions. As a result, the data may violate the independence assumption. When the independence assumption is violated, the likelihood of making a Type I (rejecting the null when it is

---

[15] The decision to over sample was left to the investigator in a given state. This decision may have stemmed from either personal interest in a specific trial, or from efforts to improve reliability.

true) or Type II error (accepting the null when it is false) increases (Kashy & Kenny, 2000, p. 458).[16]

Second, the dependent and independent variables are multilevel in nature. Victim marital status, for example, is a group level variable, and victim evaluation is a juror level variable. Most traditional multivariate statistics, e.g., linear regression, are not adequate for analyzing multilevel variables simultaneously (Williams, 1999, p. 475). Both the violation of the independence assumption and the use of multi-level variables were legitimate threats to statistical conclusion validity that had to be accounted for. Several steps were taken in response these concerns.

Testing for Independence: The Intraclass Correlation

Intraclass correlations measure the proportion of variation in the outcome measure that is accounted for by the group (Kashy & Kenny, 2000, p. 454). A large intraclass correlation can be interpreted as indicating that there is a lot of variation between different juries but only little variation among jurors within juries. The intraclass correlations for several of the study's dependent variables were computed to assess the degree of non-independence within juries.

Intraclass correlations assume that there are an equal number of participants per group. The CJP data did not meet this criterion. Consequently, groups of three were created to address this problem. Juries with less than three jurors in the sample were excluded from the analysis. A random sample of three jurors was selected from cases with four or more jurors. This procedure produced 88 juries and some 264 jurors.[17] As illustrated in Table 1, the data appear to violate the independence assumption. For example, 73 percent of the variance in victim evaluation scores can be explained by membership within a particular jury. This suggests that there is little variation on victim evaluation scores among jurors within a given case. Traditional

---

[16] The effect of non-independence on significance testing depends on the type of independent variable(s) included in the analysis and the direction of the non-independence.

[17] Some analyses included a smaller number of groups and jurors due to missing data.

multivariate analyses are likely to be biased under these circumstances when the juror is used as the unit of analysis.

Table 1
Test of Non-independence

Variable	Intraclass Correlation
Victim evaluation	.73
Empathy toward the victim/family	.31
Mitigating evidence evaluation	.39
Empathy toward the defendant/family	.03
Defendant evaluation	.38

Solution 1: Hierarchical Linear Modeling

Hierarchical Linear Modeling (HLM) is a statistical technique used to analyze data in which lower level units are nested within higher-level units (Raudenbush & Bryk, 2001). HLM accounts for non-independence within groups by computing a separate intercept and slope for each level 2 unit in the analysis, and then using this information to predict the slopes and intercept parameters of variables at the lower levels. This procedure separates the variance associated with the group from the level 1 intercept and slope. In doing so, HLM is able to account for non-independence within the units in the lower level, model multi-level variables simultaneously, and also determine if the relationship between a predictor and criterion variable varies across groups. In the first step of the analysis, a regression is conducted for each group (e.g., jury) using individual level data (e.g., juror), resulting in unique intercepts and betas for every level 2 unit. In the second step, the regression parameters from the first stage are treated as outcome variables, and level 2 variables are used to predict the coefficients.

Because HLM produces a separate regression line for each group, the analysis requires a sufficient number of observations within each unit. The average group size in the CJP sample was 3.2, which is not a sufficient number of observations for stable parameter estimates. Some researchers have recommended, under these circumstances, that a constraint be put on the model, so that the slope is not free to vary across groups. The variance among the intercepts is then used to model the non-independence in the groups (Kenny et al., 2002, p. 132). To account for the intraclass correlations identified in Table 1, a constrained HLM technique was used to test the study's hypotheses. This approach increased the power of the analysis, and reduced the likelihood that a Type I or Type II error resulted as a product of non-independence. A conservative sampling method was used as a second approach to address the threats to statistical conclusion validity. This method is described below.

Solution 2: Random Sample technique

The second approach employed to address the problem of non-independence involved randomly selecting a single juror from each jury. This eliminated the effects that interdependence and multi-level variables may have had on the final results. However, this correction resulted in a significant loss of data and power. The sample size was reduced by over two-thirds. Both the HLM technique and the single juror sample method were used and compared to test each hypothesis and accompanying predictions.

STUDY STEPS AND STAGES

Interviewing Jurors

After six revisions and two pretests, a fifty-page instrument consisting of open- and close-ended questions was developed, designed to "chronicle the jurors' experiences and thinking over the course of the trial, to identify points at which various influences may come into play, and to reveal the ways in which jurors reach their sentencing decisions" (Bowers, 1995, p. 1082; this article provides a detailed discussion of the CJP's methodology). Every interviewer attended mandatory training sessions, where the instrument and a 15-page interview guide were reviewed. These sessions also entailed mock interviews and tape recordings of completed interviews, which were used to illustrate effective and ineffective questioning strategies. In addition, interviewers were trained to read each question verbatim, and to probe specific areas and issues identified in the instrument (Bowers, 1995, p. 1082).

Face-to-face interviews were conducted in each juror's home. These interviews averaged about three hours in length, and were tape-recorded (upon consent). Jurors were guaranteed confidentiality and paid twenty dollars for their participation. Responses to specific questions from the interviews used to test the hypotheses of this study are described subsequently.

Additional Data on Case Facts

For purposes of this study case facts were used to create a scale which classified cases as to similarity on the basis of legal crime, defendant, and victim characteristics. This scale served as a control for the factual differences among cases. Data were collected on variables identified in the archival literature as predictors of final sentence outcome. These variables are identified in Table 2.

In an effort to maintain reliability, published state and U.S. Supreme Court opinions on the Lexis-Nexis database were used as the primary source for case information. However, published opinions were missing for approximately 32 cases within the CJP sample. CJP data were used as the primary source for crime facts for these cases and also to supplement published opinions when additional information was needed. When the CJP served as the primary data source, a case summary was created from juror responses to a question in the instrument that asked jurors to provide details of the crime (see Section IIA, Question 1 of the CJP interview instrument). Because juror recall was a potential threat to the reliability of the scale, a triangulation approach was developed to enhance the reliability of reported summaries. Facts that were either corroborated or not contradicted by other jurors in the sample were deemed to be reliable.

The memory of an event that is perceived to be vivid or important is more elaborated than recall of ordinary daily events (Matlin, 1994, p. 150). According to Bowers (1995), it was common for jurors to comment that the experience was "truly memorable," something that they would "never forget" because "it was the most important thing I have ever done" (Bowers, 1995, p. 1086). If the capital trial event was perceived to be an important and vivid experience, jurors' memory of the general fact pattern of the case should be fairly accurate.

Responses to close-ended questions from the interview instrument asking about the presence or absence of particular types of evidence were used to supplement case summaries, and also to supplement Lexis published opinions. A triangulation approach requiring two-thirds agreement among jurors was established as a criterion for reliability. Case summaries from jurors' descriptions, the codebook used in this study, and agreement percentages from the close-ended questions are located in Appendix B, C, and D.

Table 2
"Deathworthiness" Variables

Crime Details	**Lingering Doubt**	**Heinousness of Murder**	**Victim Details**	**Mitigation/ Diffusion of Responsibility**	**Other**
Crime scene	Confession	Victim was beaten	Peace officer	Defendant was triggerman	Crime spree
Number injured	Arrested at scene (escaping)	Bloody murder	Age (child or senior)	Multiple triggermen/ Contested issue	Prior history of violent crime
Number killed	Accomplice testimony	Multiple stab wounds		Intoxicated	
Weapon	Eyewitness	Multiple gunshot wounds		More than one offender	
Occurred during the commission of a felony	Witness (heard defendant confess)	Single cut or stab		Victim resisted	
Charge in addition to murder		Rape or sexual motive		Intentional/ Spontaneous	
Victim/offen der relationship		Torture or mutilation			
		Prior history of violence against victim			

The "deathworthiness" scale was developed by running a Kendall's Tau-B correlation matrix on all 30 variables. Twelve variables were extracted that had correlation coefficients with sentence outcome of .1 or greater, and coefficients of .25 or lower with each other. These twelve variables were as follows:

- Accomplice testimony (ACCOMPLI)
- Arrested at scene
- Eyewitness
- Witness heard confession (HEARDCON)
- Victim was a senior (SENIOR)
- Victim was a child
- Multiple gunshot wounds (MULTGUN)
- Burglary (BURGLARY)
- Number injured
- Torture/mutilation
- Intentional or spontaneous
- Scene of crime: Home/work

These 12 variables were then entered into a forward stepwise logistic regression analysis with sentence outcome as the criterion variable. Results from the final model are illustrated in Table 3. Five variables were found to be significant predictors of sentence outcome (jury penalty decision). A "deathworthiness" score was computed for each case by multiplying the presence or absence of these five legal case factors by their corresponding beta weights, and then summing the total. The Pearson correlation coefficient between the deathworthiness scale and final sentence outcome was .246, p = .004.

Table 3
"Deathworthiness" Scale Logistic Regression

		B	S.E.	Wald	df	Sig.	Exp(B)
Step 5	BURGLARY	-1.755	.610	8.272	1	.004	.173
	ACCOMPLI	-.907	.443	4.202	1	.040	.404
	HEARDCON	1.151	.474	5.906	1	.015	3.161
	SENIOR	1.614	.782	4.258	1	.039	5.024
	MULTGUN	1.459	.586	6.201	1	.013	4.303
	Constant	.134	.305	.192	1	.661	1.143

<u>Hypothesis 1:</u> The race of the victim affects white jurors' empathy toward the victim.

Unit of Analysis and Sample Size

The juror served as the unit of analysis for Hypothesis 1. For the single juror sample used to test this hypothesis, a single white juror was randomly selected from each of the 139 juries within the cleaned CJP sample. Thirty-seven cases had only one juror, eight of whom were black. These eight cases were excluded from the Hypothesis 1 sample. The 29 remaining cases met the white juror criterion, and were black. These eight cases were excluded from the Hypothesis 1 sample. The 29 remaining cases met the white juror criterion, and were included. Thus, the Hypothesis 1 single juror (SJ) sample included 131 white jurors from 131 cases. The sample for the HLM analysis included 245 245 white jurors nested within 93 juries.

<u>Prediction 1a</u>: White jurors display more empathy toward the victim and his family in interracial (black-defendant/white-victim) as compared to intra-racial (black-defendant/black-victim) homicide.

Defining and Measuring Empathy

Empathy involves relating to another person and taking his or her perspective, which invokes feelings of sympathy, compassion, tenderness, and other similar feelings (see Batson, 1991, 1997). According to the dual process model the social comparison process should accentuate empathy when the victim is a member of the in-group, and attenuated when the victim is a member of the out-group. Questions that focus on jurors' ability to take the victim's and his family's perspective; address perceptions of similarity between the juror and victim; and measure emotions that empathy is likely to evoke were used to measure empathy. Questions pertinent to empathy are laid out in Section IIC. Question 3 reads as follows, "Did you have any of the following thoughts or feelings about (Vic)_____?" Jurors were asked to indicate "yes," "no," or "not sure" to the following statements:

- Admired or respected (Vic)___
- Imagined yourself in (Vic)___'s situation
- Imagined yourself as a friend of (Vic)___
- Imagined (Vic)___as a member of your own family
- Felt grief or pity for the victim
- Disgusted or repulsed by the victim

Section IIC, Question 5, reads as follows, "Whether or not they came to trial, did you have any of the following thoughts or feelings about (Vic)____'s family?" Jurors were asked to indicate "yes", "no", or "not sure" to the following statements:

- Imagined yourself in their situation
- Felt their grief and sense of loss
- Wished you knew (Vic)___'s family personally
- Imagined yourself as a member of (Vic)___'s family
- Felt distant or remote from them
- They seemed very different from your own family

An empathy scale was created from seven items. Five of the items were used to measure jurors' ability to take the perspective of the victim and his family:

- Imagined yourself in (Vic)___'s situation
- Imagined yourself as a friend of (Vic)___
- Imagined (Vic)___ as a member of your own family
- Imagined yourself in their situation
- Imagined yourself as a member of the (Vic)___'s family

Two items were used to measure social distance:

- Felt distant or remote from them
- They seemed very different from your own family

Each item was evaluated on a three point-ordinal scale created from the response set: (1) No; (2) Not sure; and (3) Yes. An empathy score was computed for each juror by averaging his raw score responses across the seven items. The empathy scale ranged from 1 to

3. Low scores indicate low empathy and high scores indicate high empathy toward the victim and his family. A Cronbach's alpha was conducted (n =404) to test the reliability of the seven-item empathy scale. The scale was reliable, α = .74. Thus, empathy was operationalized as *jurors' ability to take the perspective of the victim and his or her family.*

Statistical Analysis

Group membership on the premise of race should be salient within the interracial and black-defendant/black-victim conditions. The proposed dual process model predicts that salience affects empathy. Prediction 1a tested the influence of race-of-victim on empathy towards the victim within conditions where race-based social comparison and in-group identification were most likely to occur. Empathy toward the victim and his family should be higher when the victim is a member of the in-group (i.e., white) than when he is a member of the out-group (i.e., black). Linear regression was employed to estimate the strength of the relationship between the criterion variable **empathy** and the predictor variable **defendant/victim racial category**. An HLM analysis was also conducted to test Prediction 1a. Because the predictor variable race is a dichotomous variable, it was not centered.

It is possible that the inter- and intra-racial homicide conditions within the sample were dissimilar from one another on several demographic variables, e.g., gender of the victim. If so, one or more of these potential confounds may account for the relationship between empathy and race. Prediction 1ai, 1aii, 1aiii, and 1aiv test these possibilities. A hierarchical regression was conducted to test the importance of defendant/victim racial category after controlling for the variables operationalized in Table 4. The control variables were entered into the first step of the analysis. The race variable was entered into step 2. An HLM analysis was also used to test the significance of race-of-defendant/race-of-victim after controlling for these variables. Because the race-of-defendant/race-of-victim, victim gender, victim children, and victim marital status variables were dichotomous, they were left uncentered. Juror socioeconomic status, which was a continuous variable, was centered on the grand mean.

Hypothesis 2: Empathy toward the victim and his family affects white jurors' victim evaluations.

Unit of Analysis and Sample Size

The juror served as the unit of analysis for Hypothesis 2, and both Hypothesis 1 samples—single juror sample (n = 131) and the HLM sample (n = 274)—were used to test Prediction 2a and 2b.

Prediction 2a: White jurors' victim evaluations are more positive when empathy toward the victim and his family is high.

Table 4
Sub-prediction 1a Variables

Variable	Variable Type	Source	Operational Definition
*Victim Gender	Discrete	CJP, Section IIA, Question 4c	Male or female
*Victim Children	Discrete	CJP, Section IIA, Question 4c	Does or does not have children
*Victim Marital Status	Discrete	CJP, Section IIA, Question 4c	Married or Single
Juror SES	Interval	CJP, Section IX, Question 8	Juror's income

**A triangulation approach was taken using the responses of all case jurors to estimate the accuracy of responses*

Defining and Measuring Victim Evaluation

Section IIC of the CHP interview was used to measure jurors' victim evaluations. The instructions for this section read, "Next, I'd like to get your personal impressions of the (Victim)____." Question 1 reads, "In your mind, how well do the following words describe (the Victim)__?"

Five of the items measured positive victim attributes. These items were as follows:

- Admired or respected in the community
- Raised in a warm loving home
- Someone who loved his/her own family
- Had a wonderful future ahead
- Was an innocent or helpless victim

Five of the items measured negative victim attributes. These items included:

- From a poor or deprived background
- A "loner" without many friends
- Had an unstable or disturbed personality
- Was too careless or reckless
- Had a problem with drug or alcohol

Each of the five positive items was rated on a four point ordinal scale: (1) Not at all; (2) Not well; (3) Fairly well; or (4) Very well. The negative items were reverse coded, so that strong agreement indicated a poor victim evaluation. Four of the items were used to measure jurors' victim evaluations:

- Admired or respected in the community
- Raised in a warm loving home
- Had a wonderful future ahead
- From a poor or deprived background

An additional item was taken from Section IIC, Question 5:

- Admired or respected (Vic)

Victim evaluation was measured using these five items. A victim evaluation score was computed for each juror by averaging his raw score responses across items. Low scores indicated a negative, and high scores a positive victim evaluation. A Cronbach's alpha was conducted ($n = 264$) to test the reliability of the victim evaluation scale.

The scale was reliable, α = .81. Thus, victim evaluation was operationalized as *jurors' description of the victim.*

A rotated varimax principal components analysis was run, which included the victim evaluation and empathy items to ensure the independence of the two measures. As indicated in Table 5, the measures maintained their independence. Three components with eigenvalues of 1.0 or greater emerged from the analysis. In addition, all of the factor loadings except for "from a poor or deprived background" were above .60.

Statistical Analysis

Prediction 2a tested the postulation that empathy toward the victim and his or her family had a positive effect on victim evaluations. Linear regression was employed to estimate the strength of the relationship between the criterion variable **victim evaluation** and the predictor variable **empathy**. An HLM analysis was also used to test Prediction 2a. Because empathy was a continuous variable, it was centered on the grand mean.

Prediction 2b: White jurors' victim evaluations are more positive in interracial (black-defendant/white-victim) as compared to intra-racial (black-defendant/black-victim) homicide.

Statistical Analysis

White jurors' empathy toward the victim and his family should be high in interracial homicide (black-defendant/white-victim), where the victim is categorized as a member of the in-group and social comparison and in-group identification are likely to occur. Prediction 2b tested the postulation that victim evaluations were more positive when the victim was a member of the juror's racial group. Linear regression was employed to estimate the strength of the relationship between the criterion variable **Victim evaluation** and the predictor variable **defendant/victim racial category**. An HLM analysis was also conducted, to test Prediction 2b. Because the race-of-defendant/race-of-victim variable was dichotomous, it was left uncentered.

If the inter- and intra-racial homicide conditions were dissimilar from one another on potential confounding variables, the relationship between victim evaluations and the race-of-defendant/race-of-victim variable may be specious. This possibility was addressed in Predictions

Table 5
Empathy and Victim Evaluation: Components and Factors

	Component		
	1 Evaluation	2 Perspective	3 Social Distance
admired or respected in the community	.821	-	-
from a poor or deprived background	.538	-	-
raised in a warm loving home	.757	-	-
had a wonderful future ahead	.781	-	-
admired or respected vic.	.740	-	-
imagined yourself in vic. situation	-	.629	-
imagined yourself as a friend of the vic.	-	.623	-
imagined vic. as a member of your own family	-	.733	-
imagined yourself in their situation	-	.758	-
imagined yourself as a member of vic. family	-	.810	-
they seemed very different from your own family	-	-	.669
felt distant or remote from them	-	-	.771

2bi, 2bii, 2biii, 2biv, and 2bv. The sub-prediction i through iv variables are operationalized in Table 4. Deathworthiness was measured using the scale developed from Lexis-Nexis published opinions and from the CJP data.

A hierarchical regression was conducted to test the importance of defendant/victim racial category after controlling for these potential confounding variables. The control variables were entered into the first step of the analysis. The race variable was entered into step 2. An HLM analysis was also used to test the significance of race-of-victim after controlling for these variables. Because the race-of-defendant/race-of-victim, victim gender, victim children, and victim marital status variables were dichotomous, they were left uncentered. Juror SES and deathworthiness score were continuous. These two variables were centered on the grand mean.

Hypothesis 3: The murder of a positively evaluated victim is more likely to result in support for a death sentence than the murder of a less positively evaluated victim.

Unit of Analysis and Sample Size

The juror served as the unit of analysis for Hypothesis 3, and both Hypothesis 1 samples—the SJ sample (n = 131) and HLM sample (n = 274)—were used to test Prediction 3a.

Prediction 3a: There is a positive relationship between favorability of victim evaluations and the probability that white jurors' pre-deliberation sentence positions will favor death.

Pre-deliberation sentencing position is an attempt to measure juror decision-making before deliberations influence these positions. This measurement point should reflect juror as opposed to jury sentencing decisions. It is important to note that the hindsight bias may affect the reliability of retrospective self-reports of this kind. This threat is compounded as the time lapse between the trial and interview date increases.

One methodological control for the hindsight bias would be to use an alternative measure point, e.g., first sentence jury vote or sentence outcome, instead of pre-deliberation sentence position. However, this solution has several drawbacks. Sentence outcome would shift the unit of analysis from the individual to the group level. This shift may confound the relationship between victim evaluation and sentence position. Jurors may be persuaded during deliberations to change to an alternative sentence decision. The pressure to conform is particularly likely to occur when the juror holds a minority position. According to the proposed dual process model, a juror or subgroup within the jury that evaluates the victim more positively than the majority is likely to favor death. However, the subgroup may conform and ultimately side with the majority in favor of life. Shifting the unit of analysis to the group level (i.e., final sentence outcome) may lead to a spurious finding that there is no relationship between victim evaluation and sentence when this occurs. Although the juror level sentence position would be a function of the victim evaluation, the final sentence vote would be affected by group level variables that attenuate this relationship.

An additional alternative would be to use first sentence vote as the measurement point. Reference to a specific time or event (i.e., first vote) may enhance the reliability of juror recall (Fowler, 1995). In their seminal work, *The American* Jury, Kalvin and Zeisel (1966) reported that first verdict vote corresponded to the final outcome between 86% and 91% of the time, concluding that the verdict is often decided before deliberations ever begin (Sandys & Dillehay, 1995, p. 176). Kalvin and Zeisel's hypothesis is premised upon the assumption that the first vote occurs before deliberations begin, which suggests that first vote is a reflection of the pre-deliberation position. This presumption is in dispute. Sandys and Dillehay (1995) found that an average of 44 minutes passed before juries took the first vote (Sandys & Dillehay, 1995, p. 186). The sample provided by the CJP supports this finding. Fifty-four percent of the jurors who reported that they remembered sentence deliberations "very well" or "fairly well", also reported that over 40 minutes lapsed before the first sentence vote was taken. Seventy-one percent reported that at least 20 minutes passed. If jurors begin deliberating before the first vote is taken, it is possible that they will shift to an alternative sentence position before the vote occurs. Thus, first sentence vote was not a valid proxy for pre-deliberation sentence position.

If the hindsight bias was affecting juror recall, there should be little variation across the three sentence measurement points: pre-deliberation, first vote, and final vote. This is precisely what was found by Bowers et al. (1998). Less than 20 percent of jurors who reported that they had taken an early sentence position also reported that they had changed that position at the end of the proceedings. However, this finding was not replicated in the cleaned CJP sample. Although there was a strong correspondence between pre-deliberation position and first vote—approximately 68 percent—only 45 percent of jurors who met the recall criteria (sufficient recall of sentence phase evidence and deliberations) reported pre-deliberation sentencing positions that were identical with the final sentence outcome. Sixty-six percent of jurors reported first vote positions corresponding to the final sentence outcome. This variability is not consistent with the hindsight bias. The hindsight bias is likely to occur when jurors cannot retrieve pre-deliberation positions from memory (see Stahlberg & Maass, 1998). It is possible that the study's recall eligibility criteria removed these jurors from the sample. Thus, it was assumed that pre-deliberation position was not significantly affected by the hindsight bias. Therefore, it was used as the criterion variable for Prediction 3a.

Measuring Jurors' Sentencing Positions: Hindsight Bias

Section IIIC, Question 2b of the CJP interview was used to measure juror pre-deliberation sentencing position, which reads as follows, "After hearing all of the evidence and the judge's instructions to the jury for deciding on the punishment, but before you began deliberating with the other jurors, did you then think (DEF) should be given…"

The response options provided included: 1) A death sentence; 2) A life (or alternative) sentence; or 3) Undecided. The life and undecided categories were collapsed to create a dichotomous variable: 1) death; or 2) less than death. This transformation was more amenable to statistical analysis and interpretation.

Statistical Analysis

The murder of a positively evaluated victim should be perceived to be more heinous than the murder of a less positively evaluated victim. Prediction 3a tested the supposition that white jurors who took early death penalty positions evaluated the victim more positively than those who supported a sentence less than death. A logistic regression analysis was used to examine the relationship between **victim evaluation** and white jurors' **pre-deliberation sentence position.** A

Bernoulli HLM analysis was also used to test Prediction 3a (for a description of the Bernoulli model see Raudenbush & Bryk, 2001). Because victim evaluation was a continuous variable, it was centered on the grand mean.

Hypothesis 4: The perceived dangerousness of a black defendant is affected by the race of the juror.

Unit of Analysis and Sample Size

The juror served as the unit of analysis for Hypothesis 4, and a paired sample was used to test Prediction 4a. There were 37 cases in the cleaned CJP sample with one or more black jurors. A single black juror was randomly selected from cases where two or more black jurors were interviewed. A paired sample was created by matching each of the 37 cases to an all white juror case with a similar deathworthiness score. Cases were also matched by the race-of-victim/race-of-defendant category. This sampling method was employed to control for the potential confounds of these variables on perceived dangerousness. A case was randomly selected when there were several all white juror cases with similar scores and values. A juror was then randomly selected from each matched case. Four black juror cases were missing aggravation and summation scores. These cases were eliminated from the analysis. The Prediction 4a paired sample consisted of 33 white and 33 black jurors.

Prediction 4a: White jurors are more likely than black jurors to describe a black defendant as dangerous to other people.

Defining and Measuring Jurors' Defendant Attributions

The Capital Jury Project did not measure jurors' defendant attributions. However, they did measure the perceived danger that the defendant poses to others. Perceived future dangerousness—likelihood of recidivism—suggests that a negative internal attribution has been made; the defendant is a dangerous individual (see Sanderson, Zanna, & Darley, 2000). However disagreement with such a statement implies that the juror did not believe that the murder was indicative of the defendant's disposition. Perceptions of dangerousness were used as a measurement of a negative defendant attribution, which was operationalized as *jurors' belief that the defendant has a violent disposition.* Section IIB Question 1, was used to measure perceived future dangerousness and reads as follows, "In your mind, how well do the following words describe the defendant?"

- ❑ Dangerous to other people

Jurors were provided with the following response options: 1) Very well; 2) Fairly well; 3) Not well; and 4) Not at all. The dispersion across responses indicated that few jurors fell within the categories, "Not very well" and "Not at all." These two categories were collapsed into a single category for the analysis. An ordinal scale was created by reverse coding juror responses as follows: 1) Not at all/Not well; 2) Fairly well; and 3) Very well.

Statistical Analysis

Black jurors are less likely than white jurors to hold an African American stereotype that encompasses a "violent crime" attribute (see Johnson, Adams, Hall, & Ashburn, 1997). As a result, they are less likely to formulate a defendant attribution hypothesis on the premise of this stereotype, or to perceive the defendant's behavior to be consistent with the "violent crime" attribute. Prediction 4a tested the postulation that white jurors were more likely than black jurors to make a negative internal dangerousness attribution when the defendant was black. A paired t-test was conducted to test for significant differences between white and black jurors on their perceptions of dangerousness.

Hypothesis 5: White jurors perceptions of the danger posed by black defendants affects their evaluation of mitigating evidence.

Unit of Analysis and Sample Size

The juror served as the unit of analysis for Hypothesis 5, and both Hypothesis 1 samples—the SJ sample (n =131) and HLM sample (n = 274)—were used to test Prediction 5a. The Prediction 5b single juror sample included 66 jurors. This sample is described in detail below. The Prediction 5b HLM sample encompassed 107 jurors nested within 63 juries.

Prediction 5a: *White jurors who describe the black defendant as dangerous to other people, are more likely than those who do not, to believe that the evidence proves that he would be dangerous in the future.*

Defining and Measuring Proof of Dangerousness

Section IIIC, Question 16 of the CJP interview was used to measure proof of dangerousness. Question 16 reads as follows, "After hearing all of the evidence, did you believe it proved that ..."

- ❑ (DEF) would be dangerous in the future

The response set included: 1) Yes; 2) No; or 3) Undecided. Due to the poor dispersion of responses across categories, the "No" and "Undecided" responses were collapsed into a single category, which created a dichotomous variable: 0) No/undecided; and 1) Yes. Thus, proof of dangerousness was operationalized as the *belief that the evidence proved that the defendant poses a threat to others.* As in Hypothesis 4 perceptions of dangerousness was defined as *jurors' belief that the defendant has a violent disposition.*

Perception of dangerousness was treated as a qualitative variable that was dummy coded. A qualitative variable with c classes is represented by c-1 indicator variables (Neter, Kutner, Nachtsheim, & Wasserman, 1996, p. 456). The excluded category serves as the reference by which the others are compared. Perception of dangerousness had 3 classes resulting in the two indicators. "Not at all/Not well" served as the reference category. The coding scheme for perception of dangerousness is laid out in Table 6.

In addition, approximately 82 percent of the jurors reported that they believed that the evidence proved that the defendant would be dangerous in the future. As a result, the distribution of the criterion variable was negatively skewed, (skewness = -2.0).

Statistical Analysis

Once a defendant attribution has been made, jurors are likely to conduct a biased search to confirm their hypothesis. As a result, the

Table 6
Dummy Coding Sequence for Perception of Dangerousness

Category	Attrib1 Variable	Attrib2 Variable
Not at all/Not well	0	0
Fairly well	1	0
Very well	O	1

evidence is likely to be perceived to prove the attribution. Prediction 5a tested the supposition that white jurors perceived the overall evidence to confirm a future dangerousness hypothesis, when this negative internal defendant attribution had been made. A logistic regression analysis was used to examine the relationship between the criterion variable **proof of dangerousness** and white jurors' **perceptions of dangerousness**. A Bernoulli HLM analysis was also used to test Prediction 5a. Because dangerousness was a nominal variable, it was left uncentered.

<u>Prediction 5b</u>: *White jurors who describe the black defendant as dangerous to other people give less weight to mitigating evidence than those who do not.*

Measuring Jurors' Evaluations of Mitigating Evidence

Section IVB of the CJP interview was used to measure mitigating evidence evaluations. Question 1 reads as follows, "I am going to read you a list of factors that might be true or present in a murder case." The list of mitigating factors included:

- ❑ (Def) had no previous criminal record
- ❑ (Def) was mentally retarded

- (Def) had a loving family
- (Def) was under 18 when the crime occurred
- (Def) was an alcoholic
- (Def) was a drug addict
- (Def) had a history of mental illness
- (Def) had a background of extreme poverty
- (Def) had been seriously abused as a child
- (Def) had been placed in a mental institution in the past but never given any real help or treatment for his problem
- (Def) was convicted with evidence from an accomplice who testified against defendant in return for a reduced charge
- (Def) would be a hardworking well behaved inmate
- Although the evidence was sufficient for a capital murder conviction, you had some lingering doubt that the defendant was the actual killer

Each factor was coded on: A) the presence or absence of the factor; and B) whether it pushed the juror towards a life or death sentence vote. A mitigation score was computed for each juror using Formula 1, where i represents the number of factors reported by the juror to be present in the case. Components A and B are discussed below.

Formula 1

$$\text{Mitigation Score} = \frac{(A1 \times B1) + (A2 \times B2) + \ldots + (Ai \times Bi)}{i}$$

Conceptually, the mitigation score represents the weight given to all of the mitigating factors listed that were present in the case, and whether this evidence was perceived to support a life or death sentence. Component A represents the presence or absence of each factor on the list and was measured as follows:

- Was this a factor in the case:

The response set included: 1) Yes; 2) No; and 3) Not sure. Responses were recoded into two categories: 1) Yes; and 0) No/not sure. Component B was used to determine if the evidence was evaluated as mitigation or aggravation. The instruction reads as follows, "Did this factor make you…" An ordinal scale was created by recoding responses:

1) Much more likely to vote for death
2) Slightly more likely to vote for death
3) Not more or less likely to vote for death
4) Slightly less likely to vote for death
5) Much less likely to vote for death

Mitigating evidence evaluation was operationalized as the *weight given by white jurors' to the mitigating factors they perceived to be present in the case.* As indicated in Formula 1, the mitigation score was continuous. In those jurors who identified at least one mitigator present, scores ranging between 1 and 3 represented jurors who gave weight to the mitigating evidence, but used it as aggravating evidence. Scores above 3 suggest that jurors gave weight to the mitigating evidence and perceived it to support a life sentence. Scores of 5 reflected jurors who gave a significant amount of weight to the mitigating evidence provided by the defendant as justification for leniency. Scores of 1 reflected jurors who believed that the mitigating evidence strongly supported a death sentence.

A mitigation score of 0 was also possible. This can be interpreted to mean one of two things. The CJP instrument asked the question, "was this a factor in the case?" It is possible that the defense did not present any of the factors identified in the CJP instrument into evidence. Thus, a score of 0 would indicate that the juror did not have the opportunity to evaluate these factors. However, this question can also be interpreted to mean that the defense presented mitigating evidence, but it was not perceived to be an important factor in the case.

Jurors often disagreed on the number of mitigating factors present. Some jurors in the same jury reported that there were no mitigating factors, while others reported that there were as many as 5. This could have been a function of poor recall, a misinterpretation of the question by some of the jurors (i.e., the issue was submitted, but was not a factor in the sentence decision), or a biased search for evidence that favors a particular position. Jurors who were not presented with mitigating evidence to evaluate were removed from the Prediction 5b sample. This was accomplished by eliminating instances where there was agreement among jurors that no mitigating factors were present. However, disagreement among jurors suggests that there may have been factors submitted into evidence. Jurors who indicated that no factors were presented but were contradicted by other jurors in the sample were recoded as: 3) Not more or less likely to vote for death.

The Sample: Addressing the Confound in Mitigating Evidence Evaluations

The instruction in Section IVB reads as follows, "...I want to ask you about factors that might have influenced your decision (sentence) in the case." Jurors were likely to report factors that influenced their final, not their pre-deliberation sentence position. Thus, the deliberation process likely affected their mitigating evidence evaluation scores. Jurors may integrate comments made during deliberations into their schemas that lend support to their pre-deliberation sentence position. Jurors who are persuaded to change their position and internalize this change may be particularly affected by deliberations. A factor such as "had a loving family" may have had little bearing on a juror's pre-deliberation sentencing position, but may have had a significant impact on his final sentence decision after deliberations. This could confound the relationship between negative internal attribution and mitigating evidence evaluations.

An effort was made to factor out the effects of deliberations. Several alternatives were examined in an effort to control statically for this confound. Some states in the sample (recommendation states) do not require unanimous verdicts. The Alabama statute, for example, calls for a majority sentence recommendation. A majority decision rule may limit the effects of deliberations, particularly if a majority is reached at the first vote. Under these conditions, the minority position subgroup does not need to be persuaded to reach a sentence verdict. Thus, their mitigating evidence evaluation scores may represent their pre-deliberation sentence position, not the final sentence decision. Although, jurors' evidence evaluations within recommendation states may not be significantly affected by deliberations, there were not a sufficient number of these cases within the sample for statistical analysis.

A second alternative was to remove from the analysis jurors who changed their sentence position during or after deliberations. Jurors who remained entrenched throughout the process were less likely to have significantly reevaluated their pre-deliberation perceptions of the mitigating evidence.[18] Thus, the effects of deliberations on their responses may have been minimal. This approach was used to control for the effects of deliberations on mitigating evidence evaluations.

Exactly 146 out of 321 white jurors in the cleaned CJP sample reported that their pre-deliberation sentence position was the same as their final sentence vote. These 146 jurors were nested within 88 juries. In addition, 56 of the 146 jurors had mitigation scores of 0, approximately seven of which were within cases where only a single juror was interviewed. As a result, their mitigation scores could not be compared to other jurors. Therefore, they were excluded from the analysis. The remaining 49 jurors with a mitigation score of 0 were evaluated as described above. This process resulted in a final sample of 108 jurors nested within 66 cases. A single white juror was randomly selected from each of the 66 cases. Approximately 57 percent of the sample's mitigation scores were in the middle of the scale (score: 3). Thus, the majority of the sample did not give any weight to the mitigating evidence. The Prediction 5b HLM sample encompassed 107 jurors nested within 63 juries. Approximately 64 percent of jurors within the HLM sample had mitigation scores of 3.

Statistical Analysis

Defendant attributions are likely to bias the evaluation of mitigating evidence. Jurors are likely to make an effort to disconfirm mitigating evidence that does not support their attribution hypothesis, or use subjective mitigating evidence to confirm their attribution. Prediction 5b tested the postulation that a white juror who reported that

---

[18] Jurors who reported that they did not change their sentence position may have been affected by hindsight bias.

"dangerous to others" described the defendant well gave less weight to mitigating evidence. Due to the dispersion across the perceptions of dangerousness variable within the Prediction 5b sample, it was dichotomized as follows: 0) Less than very well; and 1) Very well. Linear Regression analysis was employed to test the relationship between the criterion variable **mitigating evidence evaluation** and the predictor variable **perceptions of dangerous**. An HLM analysis was also conducted to test Prediction 5b. Because dangerous to others was a dichotomous variable, it was left uncentered.

Hypothesis 6: The defendant attribution process is independent of the victim evaluation process.

Unit of Analysis and Sample Size

The juror served as the unit of analysis for Hypothesis 6, and both Hypothesis 1 samples—SJ sample (n = 131) and the HLM sample (n = 274)—were used to test Prediction 6a and 6b.

Prediction 6a: The race of the victim is not significantly related to white jurors' perceptions of dangerousness.

Statistical Analysis

Prediction 6a tested the independence of the defendant attribution process from the race of the victim. Thus, it was a test of the null hypothesis. When the null hypothesis is predicted, there is an increased risk of making a Type II error, erroneously concluding that the variables of interest are not related. A Type II error would lead to a spurious finding that jurors' attributions are independent of the race of the victim, and would confirm Prediction 6a. In an effort to reduce the odds of making a Type II error, a .2 rather than a .05 alpha criterion was used.

The criterion variable, perception of dangerousness was dichotomized as follows: 0) Less than very well; and 1) Very well. This transformation was more amenable to statistical analysis and interpretation. Race-of-victim was coded as either white or black. A logistic regression analysis was used to examine the relationship between **perceptions of dangerousness** and the predictor variable **race-of-victim**. A Bernoulli HLM analysis was also used to test Prediction 6a. Because victim evaluation was a continuous variable, it was centered on the grand mean.

Prediction 6b: White jurors' victim evaluations are not significantly related to their mitigating evidence evaluations.

Statistical Analysis

Prediction 6b tested the independence of the victim evaluation process from the evaluation of mitigating evidence, which is postulated to result from the defendant attribution process. As in Prediction 6a, this was a test of the null hypothesis. Therefore, a .2 alpha criterion was used to evaluate Prediction 6b. Linear regression was employed to estimate the strength of the relationship between the criterion variable **mitigating evidence evaluations** and the predictor variable **victim evaluation**. An HLM analysis was also used to test Prediction 6b. Because victim evaluation was a continuous variable, it was centered on the grand mean.

Model Overall Path Analysis: According to the dual process model, the victim evaluation process mediates the effect of the race of the victim on white jurors' sentence positions. The defendant attribution process is predicted to bias the evaluation of mitigating evidence. Do white jurors reach their sentencing positions through the cognitive processes identified in the Dual Process Model?

To test the model overall a path analysis was conducted using pre-deliberation sentence position as the criterion variable. Predictor variables were defendant/victim racial category, empathy, mitigating evidence evaluation, victim evaluation, and perceptions of dangerousness

Unit of Analysis and Sample Size

For the reasons detailed in Prediction 5b, the mitigating evidence evaluation variable likely reflects final sentence decisions which can be affected by deliberations. However, it was included in this path analysis as a potential predictor of pre-deliberation sentence position for the following reasons. Excluding jurors who changed their sentence position to control for the confounding effects of deliberations would reduce the path analysis sample to 62. A minimum of 15 cases per measured variable has been recommended for structural equation modeling (Stevens, 1996). Loehlin (1992) reported that models with two to four factors should include at least 100 cases. Excluding jurors who changed their sentence position would produce an insufficient sample to test the proposed dual process model. Therefore, jurors who changed their sentence position were included in the analysis. Thus, mitigation scores reflected jurors who did, and those who did not, change their sentence positions. The decision was made to use the jury average score for each variable in the path analysis so that all 108 jurors who did not change their sentence positions, some of which were nested within the same jury, could be included in the path analysis. It was hoped that an average score that included those who did, and those who did not, change their sentence position would be less biased by deliberations than a single juror score that reflected a shift in sentence position. The final path analysis sample consisted of 128 cases. Missing data were corrected for via a maximum likelihood estimation process.

Measurements

A jury score was created for each of the variables identified in Table 7 by averaging the scores of white jurors within each jury. Pre-deliberation sentence position was operationalized as *the average sentence position of the group.*

Statistical Analysis

A path analysis was conducted to examine the model overall. Path analysis is a statistical technique that is used to evaluate causal relations among observed variables (Kline, 1998, p. 95). This approach allowed for a test of the causal pathways inferred from the dual process model. The model tested is specified in Figure 3. The number of observations, which is the number of variances and covariances within the model, sets the limit on the number of parameters that can be estimated. The number of parameters cannot exceed the number of observations. The model in Figure 3 has six observed variables, 21 observations, and nine parameters. Therefore, the model was *over identified*, or amenable to analysis.

Table 7
Path Analysis Model Variables

Variable	Variable Type	Nature of Measurement
Victim Empathy	Endogenous	Continuous
Defendant/Victim Racial Category	Exogenous	Discrete
Pre-Deliberation Sentence Position	Endogenous	Continuous
Mitigating Evidence Evaluation	Endogenous	Continuous
Victim Evaluation	Endogenous	Continuous
Perceptions Dangerousness	Endogenous	Continuous

<u>Model Extension to Final Sentence Outcomes</u>: Consistent with the aversive racism perspective, the relationship between pre-deliberation sentence positions and sentence outcome (final sentence verdict) is likely to be moderated by the salience of white jurors' egalitarian values and the clarity of the sentencing task. When are pre-deliberation sentence positions likely to carry over into final sentence outcomes?

To test the model extension to final sentence outcomes a path analysis was conducted with final sentence outcome as the criterion variable. Predictor variables were pre-deliberation sentence position, instruction comprehension, instruction guidance, the presence of five white-male jurors, the presence of a black-male juror, and deathworthiness.

Unit of Analysis and Sample Size

The jury served as the unit of analysis for the model extension to final sentence outcomes. The sample included 119 juries, 53 of which were

Figure 3: Dual process model of juror decision-making

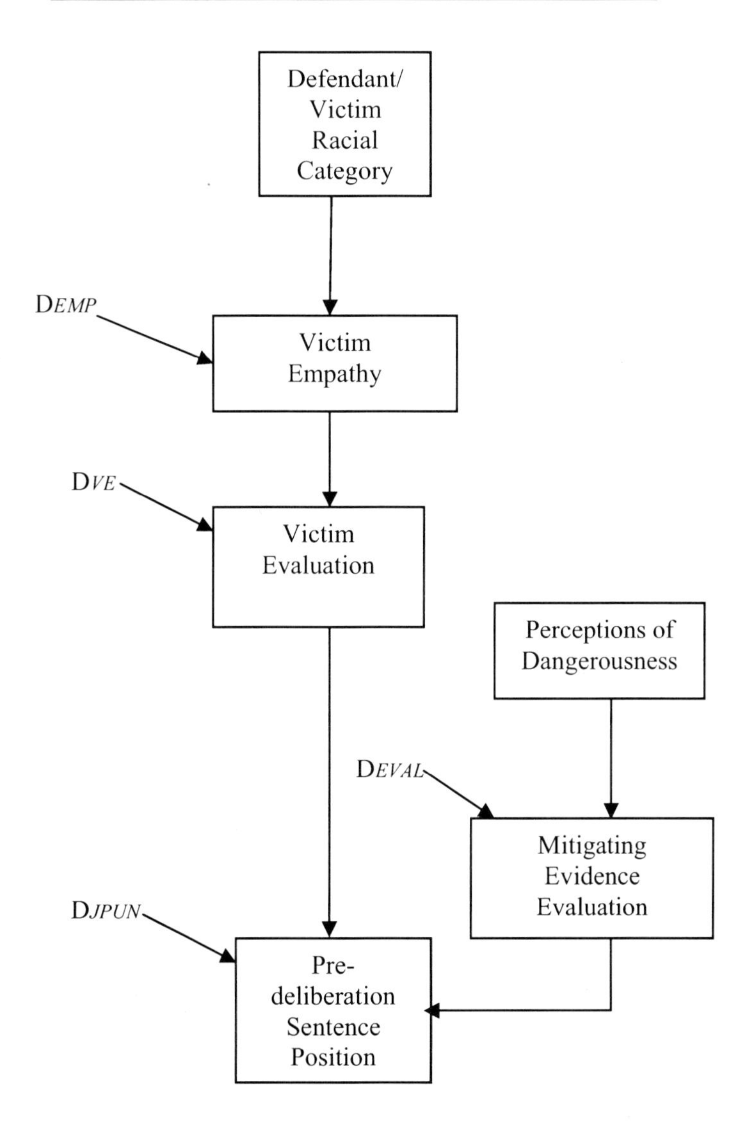

black-defendant/black-victim cases and 66 of which were black-defendant/white-victim cases.

Measurements

Six questions from Section V of the CJP interview were used to measure instruction comprehension. Due to differences across death penalty statues questions were selected for their generalizability across capital punishment systems. The six questions from Section V read as follows:

- For a factor in favor of death to be considered, did it have to be
    - Proved beyond a reasonable doubt
    - Proved by a preponderance of the evidence
    - Proved only to a juror's personal satisfaction
    - Don't know
- For a factor in favor of death to be considered, did it have to be
    - All jurors have to agree on that factor
    - Jurors not have to agree unanimously on that factor
    - Don't know
- To the best of your memory, was the jury required to impose a sentence of life or less or free to choose between death and a lesser sentence, if it found…

1) Life or less required 2) Free to choose 3) Don't know

- One or more factors opposing a death sentence and none favoring it
- Stronger factors opposing than favoring a death sentence
- An equal balance between factors opposing and favoring a death sentence

An instruction comprehension score was generated for each juror by summing the number of questions answered correctly. Jurors' scores were then averaged to create a jury score.

The variable instruction guidance was coded dichotomously as either guidance or no guidance state. Guidance states are those that provide instruction on the unanimity rule; standards of proof; how to evaluate mitigating and aggravating evidence to reach a sentencing decision; and provide decision rules (e.g., the sentence must be life if the mitigating evidence is found to outweigh the aggravating evidence). No guidance states are those that do not provide instruction on the unanimity rule, standards of proof, and provide little or no instruction on how jurors are to use mitigating and aggravating evidence. The death penalty statutes from each state in the sample were used to code instruction guidance. Thirty-nine cases were coded as guidance states. These cases were from Alabama, Pennsylvania, Tennessee, and Texas. The remaining 80 cases were coded as non-guidance states. These cases were from California, Florida, Georgia, Indiana, Kentucky, Louisiana, North Carolina, South Carolina, Virginia, and Missouri.

Jury composition was coded from Section VII, Question 10 of the CJP interview. Question 10 reads as follows:

To the best of your knowledge, how many of the 12 jurors were:

White	Black	Hispanic
#__Men	#__Men	#__Men
#__Women	#__Women	#__Women

Two variables were created: presence of a black male juror and presence of five or more white male jurors. These variables were coded for each jury by averaging the number of white and black males reported by the jurors in the sample.

The Sample and Statistical Analysis

A path analysis was conducted to examine the model's extension to final sentence outcomes. The proposed model, which is specified in Figure 4, had 7 observed variables, 28 observations, and 7 parameters. Thus, it was over identified. The variables from the path analysis are operationalized in Table 8. The analysis was run on two separate sub-samples—black-defendant/white-victim and black-defendant/white-victim cases—so that the moderating effects of race-of-victim on the paths identified in Figure 4 could be tested. The former sample included 66 cases and the latter encompassed 53. The small number of cases within each sub-sample likely affected the power of the analysis subsequently increasing the odds of making a Type II error.

Table 8
Path Analysis Model Variables

Variable	Type	Nature of Measurement	Source	Operational Definition
Instruction Comprehension	Exogenous	Continuous	Section V, Question 3, Question 4, Question 8, Question 9	Average number of correct answers within the jury
*Presence of Five or More White Male Jurors	Exogenous	Discrete	Section VII, Question 10	Yes or no
*Presence of a Black Male Juror	Exogenous	Discrete	Section VII, Question 10	Yes or no
Final Sentence Outcome	Endogenous	Discrete	Section IV, Question 14, Question 15	Life or death
Instruction Guidance	Exogenous	Discrete	State Statutes	Do the instructions detail how mitigating evidence is to be used; include the unanimity rule; and standard of proof?
Deathworthiness	Exogenous	Continuous	Lexis-Nexis CJP	Score
Pre-deliberation Sentence Position	Exogenous	Continuous	Section IIIC, Question 15	Jury average sentence position

**A triangulation approach was taken using the responses of all case jurors to estimate the accuracy of responses*

Figure 4: The effects of group level variables on jury sentence outcomes

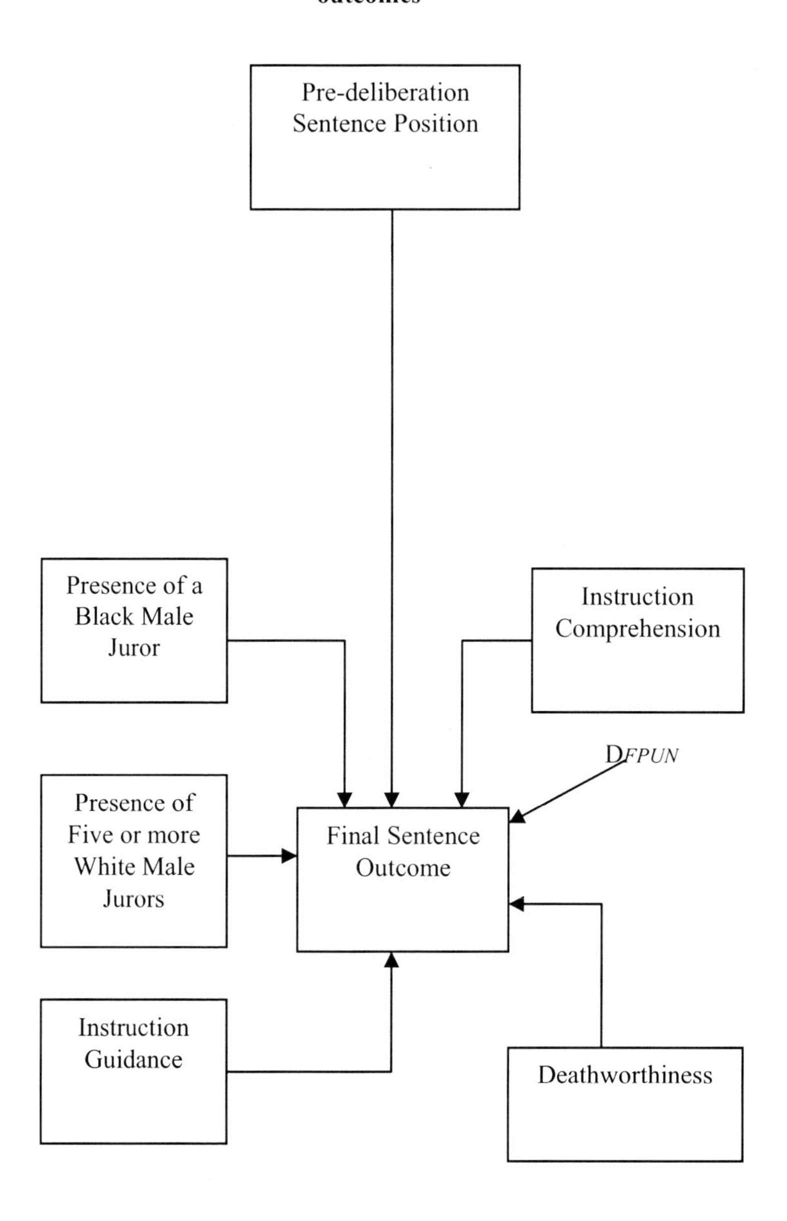

CHAPTER 7

RESULTS OF ANALYSIS AND MODELS

The HLM and single juror sample technique were used to address non-independence within each analysis when applicable. The results from these two statistical techniques are discussed below.

Hypothesis 1: The race of the victim affects white jurors' empathy toward the victim

Prediction 1a: White jurors display more empathy toward the victim and his family in interracial (black-defendant/white-victim) as compared to intra-racial (black-defendant/black-victim) homicide.

Results from the linear regression analysis are illustrated in Table 9. In support of Prediction 1a, the regression analysis confirmed that white jurors displayed more empathy toward a white than toward a black victim, $t(129) = 2.358$, $p = .02$. The presence of a white victim increased empathy by .2 units on the three-point empathy scale. The R^2 indicated that 4 percent of the variability in empathy was explained by race-of-victim.

Table 9
Prediction 1a: Empathy as a Function of Defendant/Victim Racial Category

Model		Unstandardized Coefficients B	Unstandardized Coefficients Std. Error	Standardized Coefficients Beta	t	Sig.
1	(Constant)	1.900	.074		25.569	.000
	DEF/VIC RACE	.236	.100	.203	2.358	.020

Results from the HLM analysis, which are laid out in Table 10, were consistent with those from the linear regression. The average empathy score for a white juror in a black victim case ($M = 1.82$) was lower than the average empathy score for a white juror in a white victim case ($M = 2.16$), $t(91) = 3.748$, $p < .001$. The intercept—the random effect in the model—indicated that there was significant variation in average empathy scores across juries, χ^2 (93, $N = 91$) = 119.03, $p = .03$. Therefore, it was important to take jury membership into account.

Table 10
Prediction 1a: Empathy as a Function of Defendant/Victim Racial Category

Fixed Effect for	Coefficient	Standard Error	T-Ratio	Degrees of Freedom	P-Value
Intercept	1.823192	0.079174	23.028	91	0.000
Def/Vic Racial Category	0.344468	0.091905	3.748	91	0.000

Prediction 1ai: The relationship between empathy and race is significant after controlling for the gender of the victim

Prediction 1aii: The relationship between empathy and race is significant after controlling for the marital status of the victim.

Prediction 1aiii: The relationship between empathy and race is significant after controlling for the socioeconomic status of the juror.

Prediction 1aiv: The relationship between empathy and race is significant after controlling for whether or not the victim had children.

Results from the hierarchical regression analysis supported the Prediction 1a sub-predictions. The addition of the race-of-defendant/race-of-victim variable significantly improved the model, *f-change*(1,94) = 4.532, *p* = .036. Results from the hierarchical regression are illustrated in Table 11 and 12. None of the potential confounding variables reached significance. However, the race-of-victim variable was significant, *t*(94) = 2.129, *p* = .036. The presence of a white victim increased empathy by .22 units on the three-point empathy scale after controlling for the other variables in the model. In addition, the R^2 indicated that 7 percent of the variability in empathy was explained by the model, a four percent improvement over the step 1 model. These findings were mirrored in the HLM analysis.

Table 11
Prediction 1a Sub-Predictions Step 1 Model; Empathy and Potential Confounds

		Unstandardized Coefficients		Standardized Coefficients		
Model		B	Std. Error	Beta	t	Sig.
step 1	(Constant)	2.146	.253		8.473	.000
	VICTIM SEX	1.773E-02	.103	.019	.173	.863
	VICTIM MARITAL	.220	.152	.179	1.444	.152
	JUROR SES	-3.33E-02	.052	-.066	-.646	.520
	VICTIM CHILD	-3.73E-02	.142	-.032	-.262	.794

Table 12
Prediction 1a Sub-Predictions Step 2 Model: Defendant/Victim Racial Category, Empathy, and Potential Confounds

		Unstandardized Coefficients		Standardized Coefficients		
Model		B	Std. Error	Beta	t	Sig.
step 2	(Constant)	2.066	.252		8.213	.000
	VICTIM SEX	2.893E-03	.101	.003	.029	.977
	VICTIM MARITAL	.161	.152	.131	1.056	.294
	JUROR SES	-3.88E-02	.051	-.077	-.766	.446
	VICTIM CHILD	-4.82E-02	.140	-.041	-.344	.732
	DEF/VIC RACE	.255	.120	.218	2.129	.036

<u>Hypothesis 2:</u> Empathy toward the victim and his family affects white jurors' victim evaluations.

Prediction 2a: White jurors' victim evaluations are more positive when empathy toward the victim and his family is high.

Results from the linear regression analysis are illustrated in Table 13. In support of Prediction 2a, the regression analysis confirmed that white jurors' victim evaluations increased with empathy, $t(129)$ = 5.399, $p < .001$. A one-unit increase in empathy increased victim evaluation by .43 on the four-point victim evaluation scale. In addition, the R^2 indicated that 19 percent of the variability in victim evaluation was explained by empathy.

Table 13
Prediction 2a: Victim Evaluation Predicted by Empathy

Model		Unstandardized Coefficients		Standardized Coefficients		
		B	Std. Error	Beta	t	Sig.
1	(Constant)	1.618	.220		7.350	.000
	EMPATHY	.560	.104	.432	5.395	.000

The results from the HLM analysis, which are laid out in Table 14, were analogous to those from the linear regression analysis. Victim evaluation scores increased with empathy $t(243) = 2.537, p = .011$. A one-unit increase in empathy increased victim evaluation by .16. In addition, the intercept—the random effect in the model—indicated that that there was significant variation in average victim evaluation scores across juries, χ^2 $(92, N = 91) = 641.65, p < .001$. Thus, it is important to take jury membership into account.

Table 14
Prediction 2a: Victim Evaluation Predicted by Empathy

Fixed Effect for	Coefficient	Standard Error	T-Ratio	Degrees of Freedom	P-Value
Intercept	2.791341	0.067104	41.597	92	0.000
Empathy	0.157299	0.062003	2.537	243	0.011

Prediction 2b: White jurors' victim evaluations are more positive in interracial (black-defendant/white-victim) as compared to intra-racial (black-defendant/black-victim) homicide.

Results from the linear regression analysis are illustrated in Table 15. In support of Prediction 2b, the regression analysis confirmed that the white jurors' victim evaluations were more positive for white victims than for black victims, after controlling for empathy, $t(129) = 4.11$, $p < .001$. The presence of a white victim increased victim evaluation by .32 on the four-point victim evaluation scale. In addition, white jurors' victim evaluations increased with empathy after controlling for race, $t(129) = 4.802$, $p < .001$. A one-unit increase in empathy resulted in a .37 increase in victim evaluation. Twenty-eight percent of the variability in victim evaluation (R^2) was explained by victim empathy and defendant/victim racial category.

Table 15
Prediction 2b: Victim Evaluation Predicted by Defendant/Victim Racial Category and Empathy

Model		Unstandardized Coefficients		Standardized Coefficients	t	Sig.
		B	Std. Error	Beta		
1	(Constant)	1.521	.209		7.287	.000
	DEF/VIC RACE	.475	.115	.317	4.117	.000
	EMPATHY	.479	.100	.369	4.802	.000

The results from the HLM analysis, which are laid out in Table 16, were analogous to those from the linear regression analysis. The average victim evaluation score for a white juror in a black victim case ($M = 2.43$) with an empathy value equal to the average score in the study ($M = 2.00$) was lower than the average white juror evaluation score in a white victim case ($M = 3.08$), $t(91) = 5.280$, $p < .001$.

Empathy was also found to have a significant effect on victim evaluations after controlling for the effects of race-of-victim, $t(91) = 2.527$, $p = .012$. A one-unit change in empathy increased victim evaluation by .14. In addition, the intercept—the random effect in the model—indicated that that there was significant variation in average victim evaluation scores across juries, χ^2 $(91, N = 91) = 490.46$, $p < .001$. Thus, it is important to take jury membership into account.

Prediction 2bi: The relationship between victim evaluations and race is significant after controlling for deathworthiness.

Prediction 2bii: The relationship between victim evaluations and race is significant after controlling for the gender of the victim

Prediction 2biii: *The relationship between victim evaluations and race is significant after controlling for whether or not the victim had children.*

Prediction 2biv: *The relationship between victim evaluations and race is significant after controlling for the marital status of the victim.*

Prediction 2bv: *The relationship between victim evaluations and race is significant after controlling for the socioeconomic status of the juror.*

Table 16
Prediction 2b: Victim Evaluation Predicted by Defendant/Victim Racial Category and Empathy

Fixed Effect for	Coefficient	Standard Error	T-Ratio	Degrees of Freedom	P-Value
Intercept	2.426226	0.098574	24.613	91	0.000
Def/Vic Racial Category	0.651195	0.123341	5.280	91	0.000
Empathy	0.137091	0.054251	2.527	242	0.012

Results from the hierarchical regression analysis supported the Prediction 2b sub-predictions. The addition of the race-of-defendant/race-of-victim and victim empathy variables significantly improved the model, *f-change*(5,88) = 18.961, $p < .001$ Results from the hierarchical regression are illustrated in Table 17 and 18. None of the potential confounding variables reached significance. However, the race-of-victim variable was significant, $t(88) = 3.489$, $p < .001$. The presence of a white victim increased victim evaluation by .32 units on the five-point victim evaluation scale after controlling for victim empathy and the other variables in the model. Victim empathy was also significant, $t(88) = 4.266$, $p < .001$. A one-unit increase in empathy increased victim evaluation by .43 after controlling for race and the other variables within the model. Thirty-six percent of the variability in victim evaluation (R^2) was explained by the model, a .29 percent improvement over the step 1 model. These findings were mirrored in the HLM analysis.

Table 17
Prediction 2b Sub-Predictions Step 1 Model: Victim Evaluation and Potential Confounds

Model		Unstandardized Coefficients		Standardized Coefficients	t	Sig.
		B	Std. Error	Beta		
step 1	(Constant)	2.742	.347		7.900	.000
	DEATHWORTHINESS	1.694E-02	.075	.024	.227	.821
	VICTIM SEX	8.598E-02	.137	.069	.627	.532
	VICTIM CHILD	-3.72E-02	.195	-.024	-.191	.849
	VICTIM MARITAL	.480	.213	.290	2.253	.027
	JUROR SES	-3.73E-02	.071	-.054	-.528	.599

Table 18
Prediction 2b Sub-Predictions Step 2 Model: Defendant/Victim Racial Category, Empathy, Victim Evaluation, and Potential Confounds

Model		Unstandardized Coefficients		Standardized Coefficients	t	Sig.
		B	Std. Error	Beta		
step 2	(Constant)	1.398	.392		3.566	.001
	DEATHWORTHINESS	2.478E-02	.063	.036	.394	.695
	VICTIM SEX	3.964E-02	.116	.032	.342	.733
	VICTIM CHILD	-8.87E-02	.165	-.056	-.538	.592
	VICTIM MARITAL	.277	.183	.168	1.517	.133
	JUROR SES	-1.03E-02	.060	-.015	-.172	.863
	DEF/VIC RACE	.505	.145	.319	3.489	.001
	EMPATHY	.510	.119	.381	4.266	.000

Hypothesis 3: The murder of a positively evaluated victim is more likely to result in support for a death sentence than the murder of a less positively evaluated victim.

Prediction 3a: There is a positive relationship between favorability of victim evaluations and the probability that white jurors' pre-deliberation sentence positions will favor death.

Results from the logistic regression analysis are illustrated in Table 19. The effect of victim evaluation on pre-deliberation sentence position was not significant, $W(1) = .494$, $p = ns$. A *post hoc* logistic regression was conducted that included empathy, race-of-victim, and victim evaluation. The results from this analysis are located in Table 20. While victim evaluation was not significant, the probability that a white juror would support a pre-deliberation death sentence position increased significantly with empathy after controlling for victim evaluation and defendant/victim racial category, $W(1) = 7.692$, $p = .006$. The odds that a white juror supported a pre-deliberation death sentence increased by 2.7 for every one-unit increase in victim empathy. The Nagelkerke R^2, which is equivalent to the R^2 in linear regression, was .10. The model correctly predicted 61 percent of white jurors' pre-deliberation sentence positions, an 11-percentage point improvement over the baseline, constant only model.

Table 19
Prediction 3a: Pre-Deliberation Sentence Position as a Function of Victim Evaluation

		B	S.E.	Wald	df	Sig.	Exp(B)
Step 1	VICEVAL	.167	.237	.494	1	.482	1.181
	Constant	-.476	.679	.492	1	.483	.621

Table 20
Prediction 3a: Pre-Deliberation Sentence Position as a Function of Victim Evaluation, Empathy, and Race-of-Victim

		B	S.E.	Wald	df	Sig.	Exp(B)
Step 1	EMPATHY	1.006	.363	7.692	1	.006	2.735
	VICEVAL	-.026	.290	.008	1	.928	.974
	DEF/VIC RACE	.512	.404	1.608	1	.205	1.669
	Constant	-2.226	.962	5.354	1	.021	.108

The results from the Bernoulli HLM analysis, which are laid out in Table 21, conflicted with those from the logistic regression analysis. In support of Prediction 3a, the analysis confirmed that the probability that a white juror would support a pre-deliberation death sentence position increased significantly with victim evaluation, $t(243) = 3.013$, $p = .003$. The odds that a white juror supported a pre-deliberation death sentence increased by .86 for every one-unit increase in victim evaluation. In addition, the intercept—the random effect in the model—indicated that there was significant variation in pre-deliberation sentence positions across juries, χ^2 $(92, N = 93) = 121.95$, $p = .02$. Thus, it is important to take jury membership into account.

A *post hoc* Bernoulli analysis was conducted that included empathy, defendant/victim racial category, and victim evaluation. The results from this analysis are located in Table 22. The probability that a

Table 21
HLM: Pre-deliberation Sentence Position as a Function of Victim Evaluation

Fixed Effect for	Coefficient	Standard Error	T-Ratio	Degrees of Freedom	P-Value
Intercept	-0.102012	0.150175	-0.679	92	0.497
Victim Evaluation	0.621218	0.206163	3.013	243	0.003

white juror would support a pre-deliberation death sentence position increased significantly with victim evaluation after controlling for empathy and defendant/victim racial category, $t(241) = 2.957, p = .004$. The odds that a white juror supported a pre-deliberation death sentence increased twofold for every one-unit increase in victim evaluation. Neither empathy nor race had a significant effect on the probability that a white juror would support a pre-deliberation death sentence position.

Table 22
HLM: Pre-Deliberation Sentence Position as a Function of Victim Evaluation and Empathy

Fixed Effect for	Coefficient	Standard Error	T-Ratio	Degrees of Freedom	P-Value
Intercept	-0.017356	0.254090	-0.068	91	0.679
Def/Vic Racial Category	-0.147007	0.355470	-0.414	91	0.339
Victim Evaluation	0.701350	0.237200	2.957	241	0.004
Empathy	-0.119217	0.233336	-0.511	241	0.609

Hypothesis 4: The perceived dangerousness of a black defendant is affected by the race of the juror.

Prediction 4a: White jurors are more likely than black jurors to describe a black defendant as dangerous to other people.

The results from the paired t-test are illustrated in Table 23. Prediction 4a was not supported. There was no significant difference between white and black jurors on their perceptions of dangerousness ($M_{white\ jurors} = 2.3$; $M_{black\ jurors} = 2.4$), $t(32) = .818$, $p = ns$.

Table 23
Prediction 4a: Perceptions of Dangerousness as a function of the Race of the Juror

		Paired Differences					
		Mean	Std. Deviation	Std. Error Mean	t	df	Sig. (2-tailed)
Pair 1	PERCEPTION OF DANGEROUSNESS	.1515	1.06423	.18526	.818	32	.419

Hypothesis 5: White jurors perceptions of the danger posed by black defendants affects their evaluation of mitigating evidence.

Prediction 5a: White jurors who describe the black defendant as dangerous to other people, are more likely than those who do not, to believe that the evidence proves that he would be dangerous in the future.

Results from the logistic regression analysis based on the single juror sample are illustrated in Table 24. In support of Prediction 5a, the probability that white jurors believed that the evidence proved that the defendant was dangerous increased with their perceptions of dangerousness. White jurors who reported that "dangerous to others" described the defendant "fairly well" were approximately 3.3 times more likely than those who reported "not at all/not well" to believe that the evidence proved that the defendant would be dangerous in the future, $W(1) = 4.02$, $p = .045$. In addition, white jurors who reported that "dangerous to others" described the defendant "very well" were approximately 9.4 times more likely than those who reported "not at all/not well" to believe that the evidence proved that the defendant would be dangerous in the future, $W(1) = 14.44$, $p < .001$. The Nagelkerke R^2 was .18.

Results from the Bernoulli HLM analysis (Table 25) mirrored those from the logistic regression. White jurors who reported that "dangerous to others" described the defendant "fairly well" were approximately 5 times more likely than those who reported "not at all/not well," to believe that the evidence proved that the defendant would be dangerous in the future, $t(271) = 4.23, p < .001$. In addition,

Table 24
Prediction 5a: Proof of Dangerousness Predicted by Perception of Dangerousness

		B	S.E.	Wald	df	Sig.	Exp(B)
Step 1	FAIRLY WELL	1.183	.590	4.024	1	.045	3.264
	VERY WELL	2.246	.591	14.435	1	.000	9.448
	Constant	.167	.410	.166	1	.683	1.182

white jurors who reported that "dangerous to others" described the defendant "very well" were approximately 16 times more likely than those who reported "not at all/not well" to believe that the evidence proved that the defendant would be dangerous in the future, $t(271) = 7.04, p < .001$. The intercept—the random effect in the model—indicated that that there was not significant variation in average evidence evaluations across juries, χ^2 $(95, N = 91) = 93.92, p =$ *ns*. This is likely to be the product of the negatively skewed distribution.

Table 25
Prediction 5a: Proof of Dangerousness Predicted by Perception of Dangerousness

Fixed Effect for	Coefficient	Standard Error	T-Ratio	Degrees of Freedom	P-Value
Intercept	-0.301772	0.269682	-1.119	94	0.264
Fairly likely	1.605272	0.379257	4.233	271	0.000
Very likely	2.740257	0.389340	7.038	271	0.000

<u>Prediction 5b</u>: *White jurors who describe the black defendant as dangerous to other people give less weight to mitigating evidence than those who do not.*

Results from the linear regression analysis are illustrated in Table 26. Prediction 5b was not supported. The effect of perception of dangerousness on mitigating evidence evaluation was not significant, $t(64) = 1.133, p =$ *ns*. The results from the HLM analysis (Table 27) were consistent with this conclusion.

Table 26
Prediction 5b: Mitigating Evidence Evaluation as a Function of Perception of Dangerousness

Model		Unstandardized Coefficients		Standardized Coefficients	t	Sig.
		B	Std. Error	Beta		
1	(Constant)	2.996	.123		24.364	.000
	Perception of Dangerousness	.177	.156	.146	1.133	.262

<u>Hypothesis 6</u>: The defendant attribution process is independent of the victim evaluation process.

<u>Prediction 6a</u>: The race of the victim is not significantly related to white jurors' perceptions of dangerousness.

Results from the logistic regression analysis are illustrated in Table 28. In support of Prediction 6a, race-of-victim was not significantly related to white jurors' perceptions of dangerousness, $W(1) = .440$, $p = ns$. The results from the Bernoulli HLM analysis, which are laid out in Table 29, were analogous to those from the logistic regression analysis, $t(93) = 1.321$, $p = ns$. However, the p value did not meet the .2 criterion, $p = .19$.

Table 27
Prediction 5b: Mitigating Evidence Evaluations as a Function of Perception of Dangerousness

Fixed Effect for	Coefficient	Standard Error	T-Ratio	Degrees of Freedom	P-Value
Intercept	3.142213	0.109689	28.647	62	0.000
Perception of Dangerousness	0.007770	0.118724	-0.065	105	0.948

<u>Prediction 6b</u>: White jurors' victim evaluations are not significantly related to their mitigating evidence evaluations.

Results from the linear regression analysis are laid out in Table 30. The findings did not support Prediction 6b. White jurors' mitigating

Table 28
Prediction 6a: Independence of Perception of Dangerousness from Race-of-Victim

		B	S.E.	Wald	df	Sig.	Exp(B)
Step 1	VICRACE	.235	.354	.440	1	.507	1.265
	Constant	.102	.261	.152	1	.696	1.107

Table 29
HLM: Independence of Perception of Dangerousness from Race-of-Victim

Fixed Effect for	Coefficient	Standard Error	T-Ratio	Degrees of Freedom	P-Value
Intercept	3.090753	0.066704	46.335	36	0.000
Mitigating Evidence Evaluation	-0.134794	0.083011	-1.624	80	0.104

evidence evaluations decreased significantly as victim evaluation increased, $t(59) = -2.314$, $p = 025$. A one-unit increase in victim evaluation decreased mitigating evidence evaluation by .31 on the five-point mitigation scale. In addition, the R^2 indicated that 9 percent of the variability in mitigating evidence evaluation was explained by victim evaluation.

The results from the HLM analysis, which are laid out in Table 31, conflicted with those from the linear regression analysis. There was no significant relationship between victim evaluation and mitigating evidence evaluations, $t(80) = -1.624$, $p = ns$.

Table 30
Prediction 6b: Independence of Mitigating Evidence Evaluation from Victim Evaluation

		Unstandardized Coefficients		Standardized Coefficients		
Model		B	Std. Error	Beta	t	Sig.
1	(Constant)	3.670	.271		13.553	.000
	VEVALUAT	-.225	.097	-.306	-2.314	.025

Table 31
HLM: Independence of Mitigating Evidence Evaluation from Victim Evaluation

Fixed Effect for	Coefficient	Standard Error	T-Ratio	Degrees of Freedom	P-Value
Intercept	0.030061	0.212493	0.141	93	0.888
Race-of-Victim	0.370867	0.280746	1.321	93	0.187

<u>Model Overall Path Analysis</u>: According to the dual process model, the victim evaluation process mediates the effect of the race of the victim on white jurors' sentence positions. The defendant attribution process is predicted to bias the evaluation of mitigating evidence. Do white jurors reach their sentencing positions through the cognitive processes identified in the Dual Process Model?

Path analyses tests of the models are based on the jury as the unit of analysis. The standardized path coefficients for the path analysis are illustrated in Figure 4 and summarized Table 32. The proposed model did not fit the data well, $\chi^2(10, N = 128) = 44.055, p < .001$. Although the absolute fit of the model was poor, the results from the descriptive measures of fit suggest that the model fits the data better than the independence model. The Tucker-Lewis index was .965, and the Comparative Fit Index was .983. The model accounted for 10 percent of the variance in victim empathy, 16 percent in victim evaluation, 3 percent in mitigating evidence evaluations, and 5 percent of the variance in pre-deliberation sentence positions. Several of the paths within the proposed model were significant. The race-of-victim was found to have a significant effect on empathy toward the victim, $\beta = .31$, *Critical Ratio* = 3.728, $p < .001$. In addition, empathy toward the victim was found to have a significant effect on victim evaluation, $\beta = .4$, *Critical Ratio* = 4.895, $p < .001$. Finally, mitigating evidence evaluation had a significant negative effect on pre-deliberation sentence position, $\beta = -.22$, *Critical Ratio* = -2.205, $p = .027$. The direct path from victim evaluation, a variable predicted by the proposed dual process model to have an effect on pre-deliberation sentence positions, was not significant, $\beta = .06$, *Critical Ratio* = .656, $p = ns$. The path from perception of dangerousness to mitigating evidence, although in the predicted direction, was not significant, β= -.09 *Critical Ratio* = 1.606, $p = ns$.

Table 32
Proposed Model, Standardized Regression Weights, and R^2

Path	Coefficient	Standardized Coefficient	Critical Ratio	P Value
Race-of-Victim to Victim Empathy	.288	.314	3.728	.000
Perception of Dangerousness to Mitigating Evidence Evaluation	-.093	-.16	-1.606	.108
Victim Empathy to Victim Evaluation	.575	.398	4.895	.000
Victim Evaluation to Pre-Deliberation Sentence Position	.055	.057	.656	.512
Mitigating Evidence Evaluation to Pre-Deliberation Sentence Position	-.336	-.216	-2.205	.027

Results from the Prediction 2b analysis suggest that race-of-victim may have a direct effect on victim evaluation. In addition, the results from the Prediction 6b analysis suggest that mitigating evidence evaluations were not independent of the victim evaluation process. Finally, the results from the Prediction 3a analysis imply that victim empathy, not victim evaluation, may have an impact on pre-deliberation sentence position. The proposed model was modified in accordance with these findings, in an effort to obtain a better fitting model. The standardized path coefficients for the path analysis are shown in illustrated in Figure 6 and summarized in Table 33. The overall fit of this model was good, χ^2 (4, N = 128) = 2.897, p = .575.

The descriptive fit indices were consistent with this finding. The Tucker-Lewis index was 1.00, and the Comparative Fit Index was 1. This model accounted for 10 percent of the variance in victim empathy, 28 percent in victim evaluation, five percent in mitigating evidence

Figure 5: Proposed model, standardized regression weights, and R^2

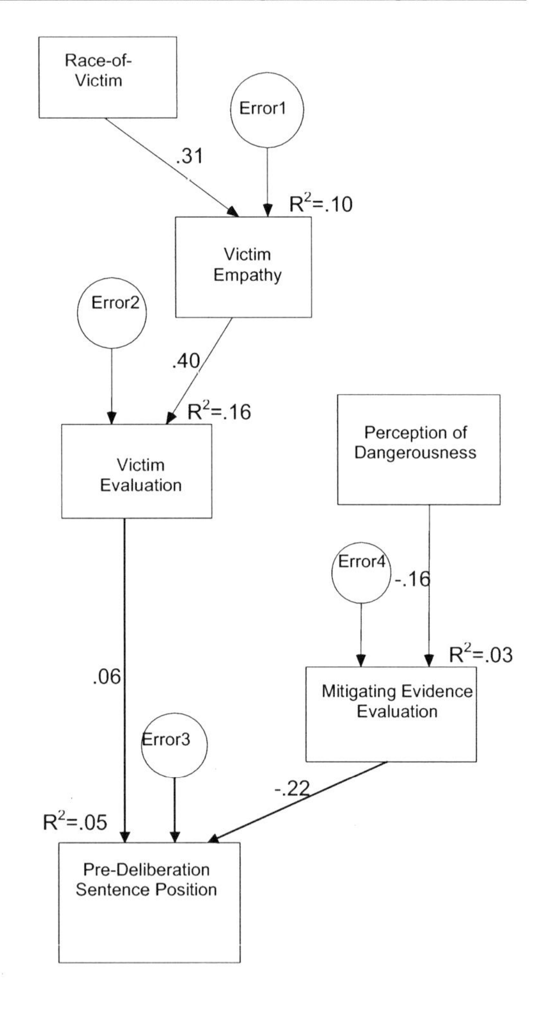

evaluations, and six percent of the variance in pre-deliberation sentence positions. Although the direct path from mitigating evidence evaluation to pre-deliberation sentence position was in the predicted negative direction, it was no longer significant, β= -.15, *Critical Ratio* = -1.502, *p* = *ns.* However, the remaining paths from the original model retained their significance. Race-of-victim was found to have an effect on empathy toward the victim, β= .31, *Critical Ratio* = 3.728, $p < .001$. The path from victim empathy to victim evaluation was diminished with the addition of the race-of-victim to victim evaluation path, but still significant, β= .28, *Critical Ratio* = 3.555, $p < .001$.

Table 33 Modified Model, Standardized Regression Weights, and R^2

Path	Coefficient	Standardized Coefficient	Critical Ratio	P Value
Race-of-Victim to Victim Empathy	.288	.314	3.728	.000
Victim Empathy to Victim Evaluation	.405	.281	3.555	.000
Race-of-Victim to Victim Evaluation	.495	.374	4.729	.000
Victim Evaluation to Mitigating Evidence Evaluation	-.144	-.233	-2.362	.018
Mitigating Evidence Evaluation to Pre-Deliberation Sentence Position	-.232	-.148	-1.502	.133
Victim Empathy to Pre-Deliberation Sentence Position	.244	.175	2.013	.044

Race-of-victim was found to have a direct effect on victim evaluations, β= .37, *Critical Ratio* = 4.729, *p* = .00. In addition, victim evaluation had a direct effect on mitigating evidence evaluation, β= -.23, *Critical*

Figure 6: Modified model, standardized regression weights, and R^2

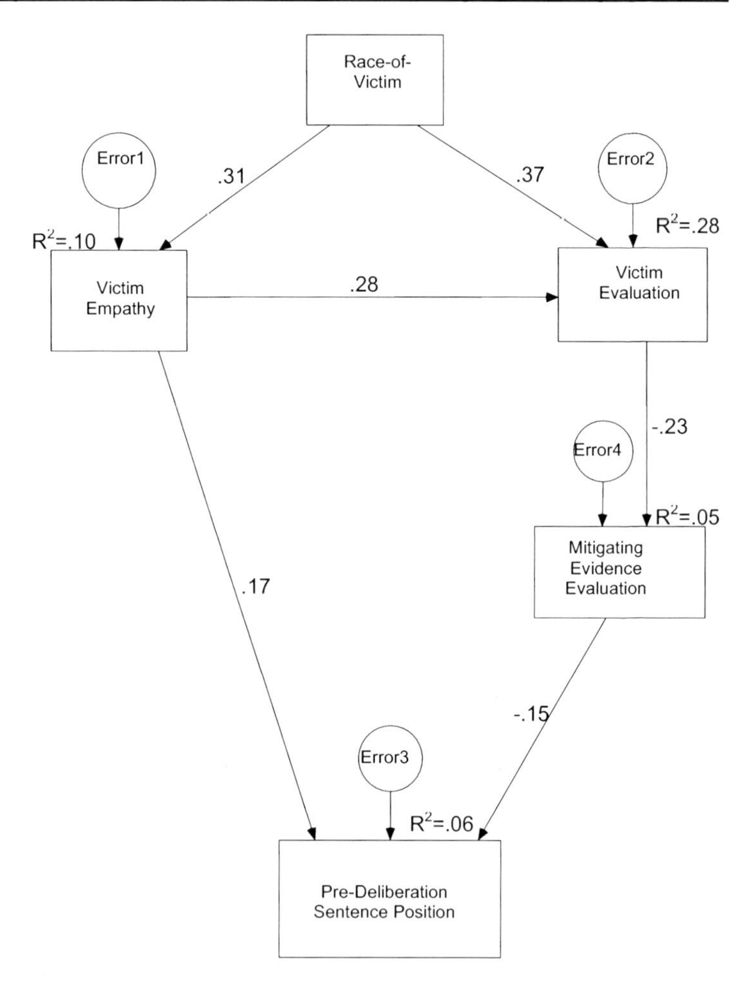

Ratio = -2.362, p = .018. Victim empathy had a significant path to pre-deliberation sentence position, β= .18, *Critical Ratio* = 3.013, p = .044. Finally, race-of-victim had an indirect effect on pre-deliberation sentence position that was mediated through victim empathy. This indirect effect was .053.

Because this *post hoc* analysis suggested that empathy had a prominent role in the decision-making process, a final modified model was developed that included two additional variables, empathy toward the defendant and defendant evaluations. A defendant empathy scale was created from Section IIB, Question 7 which reads as follows, "Did you have any of the following thoughts or feelings about (DEF)?" The response set included "yes" or "no". Two of the items were used to measure jurors' empathy toward the defendant:

- ❑ Imagined being like (DEF)
- ❑ Imagined yourself in (DEF)'s situation

Two additional items were taken from Question 9 to measure thoughts and feeling about the defendant's family:

- ❑ Imagined yourself in their situation
- ❑ Imagined yourself as a member of (DEF)'s family

A defendant empathy score was computed for each juror by totaling his or her raw score responses across the four items. Low scores indicate low empathy and high scores indicate high empathy toward the defendant and his family. A Cronbach's alpha was conducted (n = 422) to test the reliability of the four item empathy scale, α = .61. The alpha coefficient was less than the .7 criterion that has been recommended for scale construction (see Nunnaly, J, 1978).

A defendant evaluation scale was created from Section IIB, Question 1 of the CJP instrument which reads, "In your mind, how well do the following words describe (DEF)?" Six of the items were used to measure jurors' defendant evaluations:

- ❑ Sorry for what s/he did
- ❑ Someone who loved his/he family
- ❑ A good person who got off on the wrong foot

- ❑ Vicious like a mad animal
- ❑ Dangerous to other people
- ❑ Lacks basic human instincts

Each of the three positive items was rated on a four point ordinal scale: (1) Not at all; (2) Not well; (3) Fairly well; or (4) Very well. The negative items were reverse coded, so that strong agreement indicated a poor defendant evaluation. A defendant evaluation score was computed for each juror by averaging his or her raw score responses across the six items. Low scores indicate a poor defendant evaluation, and high scores indicate a positive defendant evaluation. A Cronbach's alpha was conducted (n = 326) to test the reliability of the scale. The scale was reliable, α = .70. A final defendant evaluation score was computed for the jury by averaging jurors' scores.

Several respecifications were made to the model, which included an indirect path from victim empathy to pre-deliberation sentence position. This path was mediated by defendant evaluation. The standardized path coefficients for the path analysis are illustrated in Figure 7 and summarized Table 34. The overall fit of this model was good, χ^2 (13, N = 128) = 21.223, p = .069. The descriptive fit indices were consistent with this finding. The Tucker-Lewis index was .992, and the Comparative Fit Index was .996.

This *post hoc* model accounted for 10 percent of the variance in victim empathy, 28 percent in victim evaluation, 5 percent in mitigating evidence evaluations, 9 percent in defendant evaluations, and 15 percent of the variance in pre-deliberation sentence positions.

The paths that were retained from the prior model were either significant or approached significance. In addition, all of the revised paths were significant. Empathy toward the defendant had a positive effect on defendant evaluations, β= .19, *Critical Ratio* = -2.180, p = .029. In addition, the effect from defendant empathy to pre-deliberation sentence position appears to have been mediated through defendant evaluations. This indirect effect was -.08

Empathy toward the victim reduced defendant evaluations, β= -.228, *Critical Ratio* = -2.691, p = .007. Defendant evaluation had a direct negative influence on pre-deliberation sentence position, β= -.35, *Critical Ratio* = -4.255, p < .001. The indirect effect of victim empathy on pre-deliberation sentence position through defendant evaluation was

.08. The negative path between mitigating evidence evaluations to pre-deliberation sentence position was marginally significant, β= -.16, *Critical Ratio* = -1.713, p = .087.

Table 34
Modified Model, Standardized Regression Weights, and R^2

Path	Coefficient	Standardized Coefficient	Critical Ratio	P Value
Race-of-Victim to Victim Empathy	.288	..314	3.728	.000
Victim Empathy to Victim Evaluation	.405	.281	3.555	.000
Race-of-Victim to Victim Evaluation	.495	.374	4.729	.000
Defendant Empathy to Defendant Evaluation	.134	.185	2.180	.029
Victim Empathy to Defendant Evaluation	-.254	-.228	-2.691	.007
Victim Evaluation to Mitigating Evidence Evaluation	-.143	-.232	-2.352	.019
Mitigating Evidence Evaluation to Pre-Deliberation Sentence Position	-.249	-.159	-1.713	.087
Defendant Evaluation to Pre-Deliberation Sentence Position	-.440	-.349	-4.255	.000

Figure 7: Modified model, standardized regression weights, and R^2

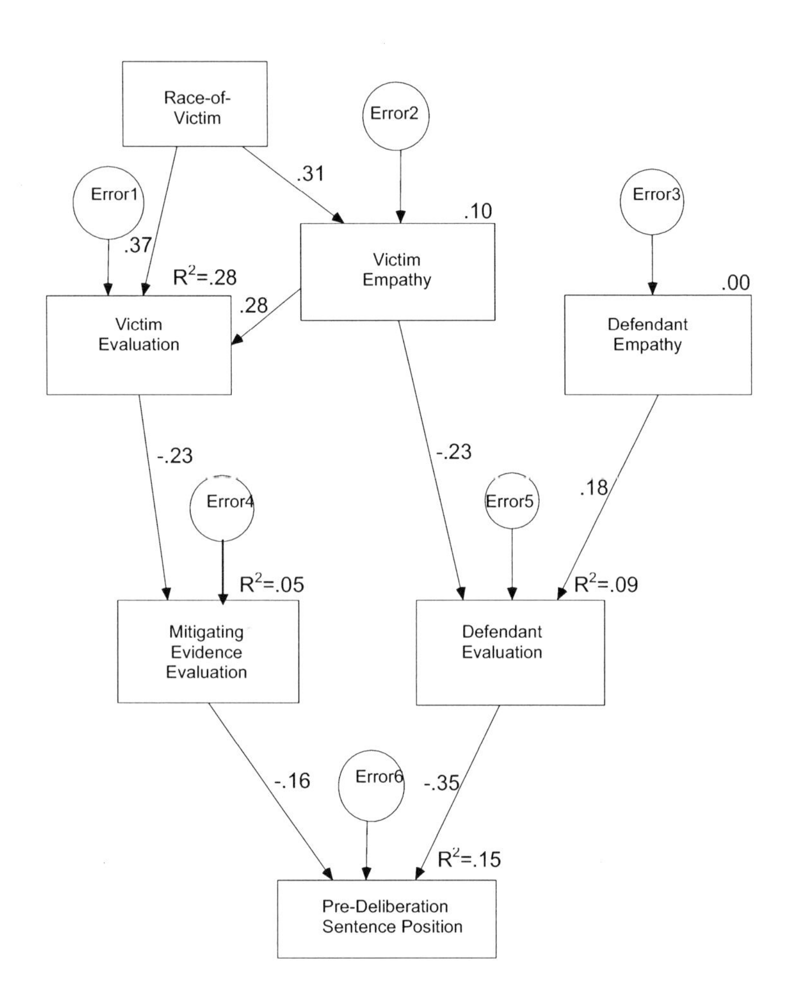

Two additional indirect paths were discovered. First, race-of-victim had an indirect effect on defendant evaluations that was mediated through victim empathy, which was .07. Race of the victim also had an indirect effect on mitigating evidence evaluations that was mediated through victim evaluation. This effect was .09.

Model Extension to Final Sentence Outcomes: Consistent with the aversive racism perspective, the relationship between pre-deliberation sentence positions and sentence outcome (final sentence verdict) is likely to be moderated by the salience of white jurors' egalitarian values and the clarity of the sentencing task. When are pre-deliberation sentence positions likely to carry over into final sentence outcomes?

All tests of models predicting sentence outcomes (final sentence verdicts) employ the jury as the unit of analysis. The first path analysis was run on the black-defendant/white-victim sub-sample. This sub-sample was selected because the race of the victim was predicted to moderate the relationship between the predictor variables and sentence outcome. The standardized path coefficients for the path analysis are illustrated in Figure 8 and summarized Table 35. The overall fit of this model was good, χ^2 (15, N = 66) = 23.667, p = .071. The descriptive fit indices were consistent with this finding. The Tucker-Lewis index was .969, and the Comparative Fit Index was .983. The model accounted for 26 percent of the variance in sentence outcomes.

Several of the paths within the proposed model were significant. The presence of a black juror reduced the likelihood that a death sentence would ensue, β= -.28, *Critical Ratio* = -2.511, p = .012. The path between deathworthiness and sentence outcome was also significant, β= .30, *Critical Ratio* = 2.795, p = .005. None of the remaining paths from instruction guidance, instruction comprehension, pre-deliberation sentence position or presence of five or more white males to sentence outcome were significant. However, both pre-deliberation sentence position and the presence of five or more white males were marginally significant. A pre-deliberation sentence position favoring death increased the likelihood that a death sentence would be handed down, β= .19, *Critical Ratio* = 1.807, p = .071. The presence of five or white males decreased the likelihood that a black defendant would be sentenced to death for killing a white victim, β= -.19, *Critical Ratio* = -1.766, p = .077.

Table 35
Relationship Between Pre-Deliberation Sentence Position and Sentence Outcome for Black-Defendants/White-Victims

Path	Coefficient	Standardized Coefficient	Critical Ratio	P Value
One Black Male Juror to Sentence Outcome	-.276	-.275	-2.511	.012
Five or More White Male Jurors to Sentence Outcome	-.192	-.191	-1.766	.077
Instruction Comprehension to Sentence Outcome	-.043	-.079	-.723	.469
Instruction Guidance to Sentence Outcome	.135	.127	1.16	.246
Pre-Deliberation Position to Sentence Outcome	.159	.193	1.807	.071
Deathworthiness to Sentence Outcome	.129	.299	2.795	.005

The second path analysis tested the proposed model on the black-defendant/black-victim sub-sample. Results from the path analysis are identified in Figure 9 and summarized Table 36. The proposed model fit the data, χ^2 (15, N = 53) = 19.969, p = .173. The Tucker-Lewis index was .977, and the Comparative Fit Index was .988. The model accounted for 18 percent of the variance in sentence outcomes. As expected, the only path that reached significance was between pre-deliberation sentence position and sentence outcome, β= .38, *Critical Ratio* = 3.044, p = .002.

Figure 8: Relationship between pre-deliberation sentence position and sentence outcome for black-defendants/white-victims

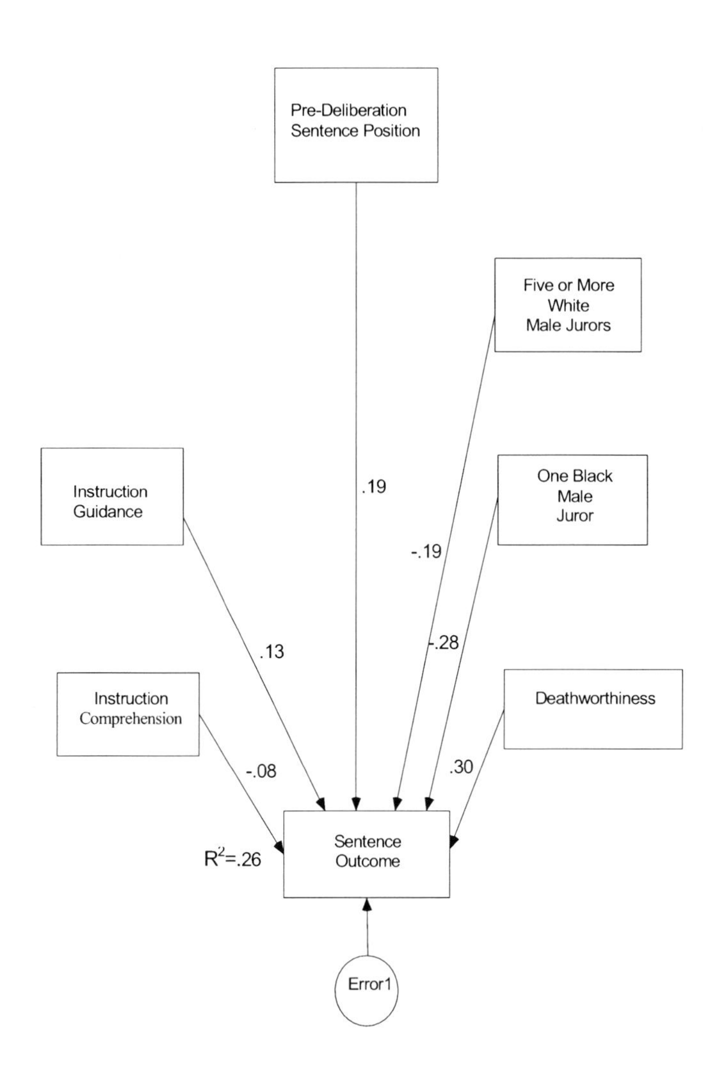

Table 36
Relationship between Pre-Deliberation Sentence Position and Sentence Outcome for Black-Defendants/Black-Victims

Path	Coefficient	Standardized Coefficient	Critical Ratio	P Value
One Black Male Juror to Sentence Outcome	-.118	-.118	-.921	.357
Five or More White Male Jurors to Sentence Outcome	-.05	-.049	-.394	.694
Instruction Comprehension to Sentence Outcome	.061	.125	.981	.327
Instruction Guidance to Sentence Outcome	.058	.058	.441	.659
Pre-Deliberation Position to Sentence Outcome	.304	.382	3.044	.002
Deathworthiness to Sentence Outcome	.013	.033	.262	.793

Figure 9: Relationship between pre-deliberation sentence position and sentence outcome for black-defendants/black-victims

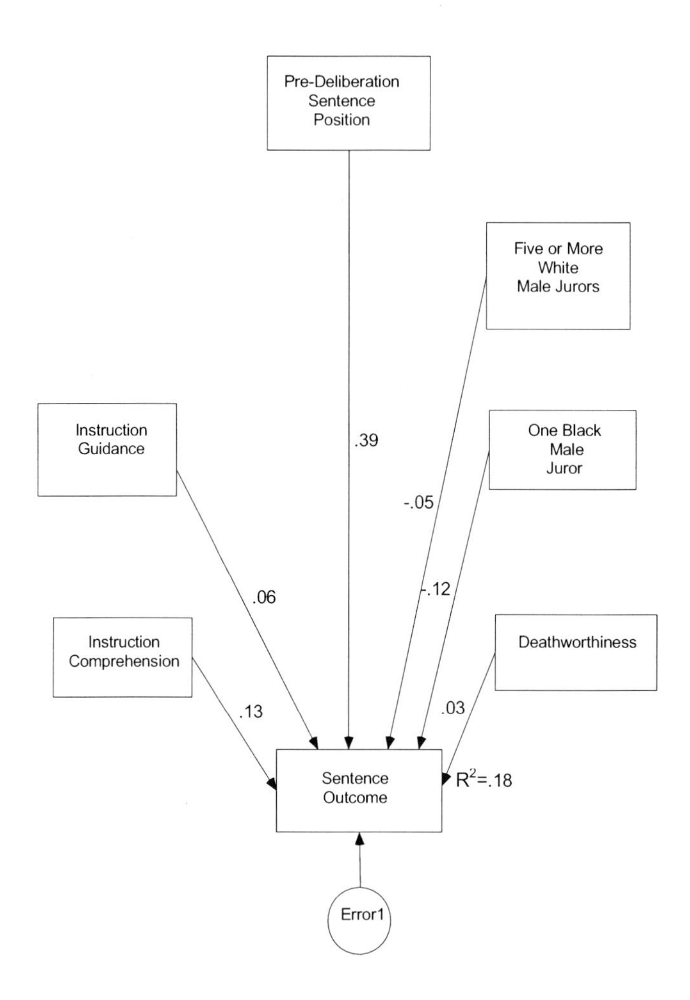

CHAPTER 8

DISCUSSION OF JUROR DECISION-MAKING: WHAT DOES IT ALL MEAN?

The CJP data offer mixed support for the proposed dual process model. Although not all of the predictions were confirmed, several extralegal factors, including race, were found to have an influence on how evidence was evaluated and ultimately how decisions were made.

THE PROPOSED MODEL'S PREDICTIONS AND SHORTCOMINGS

Regarding the victim evaluation process, and predicted by Hypothesis 1, white jurors were found to empathize more with white than black victims. In addition, consistent with Hypothesis 2, victims were evaluated more positively when empathy was high. However, the relationship between victim evaluation and pre-deliberation sentence was unclear. Hypothesis 3 was confirmed by the HLM analysis. Positive victim evaluations increased the odds that a juror would support a death sentence. However, this finding was not replicated with the single juror sample. In fact, the results from the logistic regression suggest that positive empathy, not victim evaluations, increased the odds that a juror leaned toward death before deliberations began.

Support for the defendant attribution process was limited at best. Hypothesis 4 was not confirmed. White jurors were not more likely than black jurors to report that the defendant was dangerous to others. In addition, Prediction 5b, which asserted that perceptions of dangerousness would reduce the weight white jurors gave to mitigating evidence, was also rejected. However, consistent with Prediction 5a, white jurors were more likely to report that the evidence proved that the defendant posed a continuing threat when they perceived the defendant to be dangerous to others.

The dual process model posited that the victim evaluation process was independent from the defendant attribution process. This supposition was not supported. The race of the victim was assumed to have no role in the formation of a defendant attribution hypothesis. This was confirmed in Prediction 6a. White jurors did not perceive a black defendant who had killed a white victim to be more dangerous than a black defendant who killed a black victim. However, the model also postulated that the victim evaluation process would not have an effect on the evaluation of mitigating evidence. This supposition was rejected in the Prediction 6b analysis. The weight given to mitigating evidence decreased as victim evaluations increased. Results from the Prediction 5a analysis suggest that defendant attributions may have an effect on perceptions of aggravating evidence. However, the Prediction 6b analysis implies that the victim evaluation process, not the defendant attribution process, influences the evaluation of mitigating evidence.

JURORS' PRE-DELIBERATION SENTENCING POSITIONS

Consistent with the findings described above, several of the relationships developed in the proposed dual process model were confirmed in the path analysis; however, others were not. Empathy was asserted to have a positive influence on victim evaluations. In addition, race was anticipated to serve as the basis of group categorization in interracial cases with white victims and in black-defendant/black-victim cases. It was predicted that white jurors would evaluate victims in the former category more positively than those in the latter. All of these expectations were confirmed. The model also supposed that the victim evaluation process would affect jurors' sentence positions. Specifically, the likelihood that a white juror would hold a pre-deliberation death sentence position was expected to increase with their victim evaluations. Once again, there was no support for a victim evaluation/pre-deliberation sentence position relationship. Victim evaluations did not affect pre-deliberation sentence positions.

The model also postulated that an independent defendant attribution process would occur that would affect jurors' evaluations of mitigating evidence. Jurors were expected to either discount or incorrectly use this evidence as aggravation when a negative internal attribution was made. As in the Prediction 5b analysis, perception of dangerousness was not found to have an influence on white jurors' mitigating evidence evaluations. However, these evaluations were found to influence pre-deliberation sentence positions. White jurors leaned toward life when they gave weight to the mitigating evidence proffered by the defense.

FINAL SENTENCE OUTCOMES

The effects of race on white jurors' pre-deliberations positions were expected to be most pronounced in the interracial category. As a result, these positions should be susceptible to change during deliberations. The relationship between pre-deliberation position and sentence outcome was predicted to be moderated by the clarity of the normative structure governing the sentencing task, and the salience of white jurors' egalitarian values. In accordance with the aversive racism perspective, the effect of pre-deliberation position on sentence outcome was found to be stronger in black-defendant/black-victim cases than it was in black-defendant/white-victim case. In fact, it was only marginally significant in the latter. It was also predicted that variables that either bring racial tension to the forefront or influence the development of the normative structure would have a stronger effect on sentence outcome within interracial crimes. Consistent with this hypothesis, the presence of a black male juror reduced the likelihood that a defendant would be sentenced to death in the black-defendant/white-victim condition. In fact, the path from black male juror to sentence outcome was stronger than the one from pre-deliberation sentence position to sentence outcome. However, the presence of black male jurors had no influence on sentencing in black-defendant/black-victim cases. The deathworthiness score was also found to have an influence on sentencing in interracial crimes. The likelihood that a defendant would be sentenced to death increased as the number of legal factors within the scale found to support death increased, and the number of factors found to support life decreased. However, deathworthiness had no bearing on sentencing when the victim was black. None of the remaining group variables—instruction guidance, five or more white male jurors, or instruction comprehension—had a significant influence on sentencing. However, the presence of five or more white males was marginally significant. In addition, this variable's influence on sentence outcomes was not in the expected direction. The presence of five or white males decreased the likelihood that a death sentence would occur.

COMPATIBILITY WITH THE EXISTING LITERATURE

The focus of sentence phase evidence on the cause of the defendant's behavior and on the value of the victim's life was predicted to result in independent defendant attribution and victim evaluation processes. There is support in the archival and experimental literature for race-of-victim and race-of-defendant effects that are mediated through these two processes. However, the current study calls some of the findings of these studies into question. Results that conflict and coalesce with the literature are described below.

The dual process model postulated that white jurors were more likely than black jurors to hold a stereotype of African Americans that contained a violent crime attribute. Although the CJP data did not allow for a direct measurement of stereotypes or attributions, white jurors were not more likely than black jurors to perceive a black defendant to be dangerous. This does not comport with the experimental literature on race and sentencing, which has shown that study participants punish defendants more punitively when a crime is consistent with the offender's racial stereotype (see Mazzella & Feingold, 1994; Bodenhausen & Wyer, 1985).

Jurors were also expected to integrate evidence that was consistent with their attributions into their defendant schema, and disregard evidence that did not comport with their attributions. However, neither perceptions of future dangerousness nor defendant evaluations were found to have any effect on the weight white jurors' gave to mitigating evidence. Once again, this conflicted with some of the literature. Stereotype expectations have been shown to bias information processing in a confirmatory manner (see Hamilton & Sherman, 1994). In addition, participants tend to make a cognitive effort to disconfirm arguments that are inconsistent with an attitude position. (see Edwards & Smith, 1996). Although the current results are incongruous with these studies, it is important to note that there was disagreement within juries on the number of mitigating factors present. Consistent with a confirmation bias theory, jurors may not have stored evidence into memory that was perceived to conflict with their stereotype expectancies and attribution judgments.

Research in the realm of inter-group relations suggests that in-group members are liked more than out-group members (see Sachdev & Bourhis, 1991). Mullen et al. (1992) reported that in-group members are also evaluated more positively than out-group members. Consistent with this literature, victims were evaluated more positively when they were members of the in-group. However, the attempt to expand the in-group bias effect to sentencing failed. Victim evaluations did not have the impact on white jurors sentencing positions that in-group biases would suggest. This finding may have been the result of an inadequate measurement of victim evaluations.

The duality assumption of the model was premised on data from the experimental and archival literature. Greene et al. (1998) reported that the victim did not influence ratings of the defendant or aggravating circumstances. Lynch and Haney (2000) did not find any main or interaction effects for the race-of-victim on punishment. However, the race of the defendant was found to have an effect on the way participants reacted and used mitigating information. Finally, Baldus et al. (1998) reported that the race of the victim had no bearing on the weight jurors gave to mitigating evidence; however, the race of the defendant did impact these evaluations. The current study did not support a dual process theory. Victim evaluations, not perceptions of dangerousness, were found to influence how jurors interpreted and weighed mitigating factors. This finding, coupled with the impact of race-of-victim on victim evaluations, suggests that killers of white victims had a more difficult time convincing white jurors to take mitigating factors into account than killers of blacks.

The relationship between pre-deliberation sentence positions and sentence outcomes was developed from the aversive racism perspective. The salience of race was expected to push white jurors' pre-deliberation sentence positions toward death. However, race salience during deliberations was predicted to have the opposite effect. Thus, final sentence votes were expected to be more lenient than pre-deliberation sentence positions. Consistent with aversive racism, the salience of racial tension appears to have moderated the effects of race on sentencing. White jurors were more likely to change their sentence positions in interracial crimes, where racial tension is likely to be at its peak. However, several variables predicted to affect the development of the normative structure of the sentencing task and the salience of white jurors' egalitarian values had no relation to sentencing. Lynch and Haney (2000) reported that race affected sentence decisions when instruction comprehension was low and evidence unclear. This was not supported. However, this finding is consistent with Foglia's (2003) research, which did not find a significant relationship between instruction comprehension and final sentence votes.

Bowers et al. (2001) identified two jury composition effects, "white male dominance" and "black male presence." The presence of five or more white males was reported to have increased the odds that a defendant would be sentenced to death in an interracial murder (black-defendant/white-victim). The presence of a black male was reported to have decreased the odds. There was mixed support for jury composition effects in this study. The "black male presence" effect was confirmed. Black defendants who killed white victims were less likely to be sentenced to death when a black male juror was on the jury. However, there was no evidence of a "white male dominance" effect. In fact, the presence of five or white males had the opposite effect, in that it was less likely to result in death. It is important to note that the sub-samples of black-defendant/black-victim and black defendant/white-victim cases used to test for group level effects did not meet the minimum 15 subjects per variable that has been recommended for path analyses (see Stevens, 1996; Loehlin, 1992). These effects may have been significant with a larger sample. In addition, the "liberation hypothesis" could not be tested with the current data. There were not a sufficient number of cases within the midrange of the deathworthiness scale to examine race effects within cases with ambiguous evidence.

Some of the CJP data support the literature on race and sentencing. The subtle race-of-victim effect that has been reported in the archival literature did appear to influence sentencing. However, the race effects that have been documented in the experimental literature were not uncovered within the current study. It is possible that the cognitive processes found to drive sentencing in the laboratory do not occur in the courtroom. However, it is also reasonable to assume that the limitations in the current data did not allow for a test of the types of race-of-defendant effects that have been reported in the experimental literature. Without a more direct measure of defendant attributions and jurors' stereotypes and the actual variation of defendant race, these issues cannot be resolved.

THE REVISED MODEL OF JUROR DECISION-MAKING

A *post hoc* model was developed that was premised on the paths from the proposed dual process model that were found to be significant and on the results from the hypotheses tested. This settled some of the contradictions from the Prediction 3a analyses. White jurors' empathy toward the victim, not their evaluations of the victim, appears to have influenced their sentence positions. A second *post hoc* model was developed around this finding, which added defendant empathy and defendant evaluation variables to the analysis.

Empathy toward the offender has been found to influence experimental participants' evaluations, attributions, and sentencing positions. When empathy toward the offender is high, participants are less likely to attribute responsibility to the offender (Sulzer & Burglass, 1968). Davis and Aderman (1979) reported that individuals who empathized with the defendant attributed less causal responsibility for a stabbing. Johnson, Simmons, Jordan, MacLean, Taddei, Thomas, Dovidio, and Reed (2002) found that, in comparison to participants in the low empathy condition, those in the high empathy condition were more likely to make situational attributions and more lenient punishment recommendations. Furthermore, the race-of-offender moderated white participants' empathy toward the offender. Empathy toward the victim has also been shown to influence these decisions. Deitz et al. (1982) found that participants with high levels of rape victim empathy recommended higher prison sentences, were more certain of guilt, and attributed more responsibility to the offender and less to the victim.

Both defendant and mitigating evidence evaluations were found to have had an attenuating effect on sentence positions in the empathy-based *post hoc* model. White jurors favored leniency when they saw the defendant in a positive light. In addition—although the path from mitigating evidence to sentence positions was only marginally significant—jurors were less likely to support a death sentence when they gave weight to mitigating factors.

Although empathy toward the defendant was found to affect defendant evaluations, victim empathy had a far grater influence on the decision-making process. Empathy toward the victim had a direct influence on defendant evaluations. Offenders were evaluated less positively when empathy was high. Empathy toward the victim also had an indirect effect on how mitigating evidence was used, that was mediated through victim evaluations. Mitigating evidence was more likely to be discarded or perceived as aggravation when the victim was evaluated positively. Neither white jurors' empathy toward the defendant, nor their evaluations of the defendant had any relation to how this evidence was weighed.

Consistent with the in-group bias effect, race-of-victim had a subtle influence on sentencing. In-group identification is associated with enhanced in-group evaluation, not out-group derogation (see Ryen & Kahn, 1975). Race did not have a direct effect on white jurors' pre-deliberation sentence positions. However, race had an indirect effect on how mitigating evidence was perceived, that operated through its influence on empathy and subsequent victim evaluations. Victims who were members of the in-group were evaluated more positively than victims who were members of the out-group. As a result, white jurors were more likely to discount mitigating evidence that would justify a life sentence when the victim was white. This finding comports with some of the recent research. Brewer (2004) reported that black jurors were more receptive to mitigating evidence than white jurors, particularly in the white-victim/black-defendant condition, where group membership is most salient. It is possible that a similar process is taking place here.

Race also had an indirect effect on the evaluation of the defendant that was mediated through empathy toward the victim. Jurors empathized more with the victim when she was a member of the in-group than when she was a member of the out-group. As a result, killers of whites were evaluated less positively than killers of blacks. These two indirect effects suggest that white jurors were less likely to hold a life sentence position when a black defendant was convicted for murdering a white victim.

These findings have several important implications pertaining to a defendant's constitutional rights to a trial free of racial bias and prejudice. In *McCleskey,* the Supreme Court ruled that an appellant must provide evidence of intentional and purposeful discrimination to prove successfully that his Fourteenth Amendment rights have been violated. Jurors' decisions appear to be influenced by their victim and defendant evaluations, which are either directly or indirectly influenced by race. However, the subtle influence of race on this process that was uncovered by the *post hoc* model is unlikely to meet the standard of proof set forth in *McCleskey.*

Decisions such as *Zant v. Stephens,* which have expanded the role of non-statutory aggravating evidence, may exacerbate the effects of race. Because defendant and mitigating evidence evaluations are affected by empathy toward the victim and ensuing victim evaluations, evidence that cultivates this type of empathy will ultimately limit the importance of the defendant's life circumstances on jurors' sentencing decisions. Victim impact statements are likely to have a significant influence on the evaluation of mitigating factors, through their effect on victim evaluations (see Greene et al., 1998), and may also reduce white jurors' defendant evaluations by arousing empathy toward the victim and his or her family. In the well publicized trial of Scott Peterson, Sharon Rocha testified for over thirty minutes. Sitting in front of a picture of her daughter, she berated the defendant for, among other things, leaving his wife at sea, knowing she had a problem with motion sickness—"You knew she would be sick for the rest of eternity and you did that to her anyway" (Murphy, 2004) Legal experts, journalists, and jurors reportedly broke down into tears. It is hard to fathom that such emotional testimony will not cultivate juror empathy and sympathy.

In *Payne,* the Court stated that, "victim impact evidence is not offered to encourage comparative judgments—for instance, that the killer of a hardworking, devoted parent deserves the death penalty, but that the murderer of a reprobate does not." In conflict with the Court's assurances, this study suggests that a comparative process may ensue that, to put it in Rehnquist's words—implies that the killer of a hardworking devoted *white* parent deserves the death penalty, but the killer of a hardworking *black* parent does not.

LIMITATIONS AND FUTURE RESEARCH IDEAS

The CJP data did not include a general defendant attribution measure. As a result, perception of dangerousness, which was presumed to be an example of an internal attribution, was used. The dataset was also limited to black defendants. Because of these limitations, the current data did not allow for a direct test of the defendant attribution process. This may have led to a specious conclusion that defendant attributions do not affect subsequent mitigating evidence evaluations. In addition, the survey instrument did not include an overall victim evaluation item. Rather, jurors were asked to determine if declarative statements, e.g., raised in a warm loving home, described the victim well. This limited measurement may have resulted in an erroneous finding that victim evaluations do not have a direct impact on sentencing. Most importantly, the current study is limited by jurors' ability to recall their affective reactions and evaluations of the actors and evidence at the time of trial. Many of the constructs identified in the dual process model (e.g., empathy) are state not stable cognitive phenomena. Jurors' inability to recall their cognitive and affective reactions may have tainted the reliability or validity of the data and the ensuing results. Finally, the small sample size in some of the analyses may have reduced the power of the test to detect differences and relationships between variables.

The current study did not allow for a complete examination of the proposed model. The nature of the data also precluded an examination of the causal links proposed by the model. Several of the relationships and predictions put forth in the dual process model could be clarified with future research. First, the inclusion of both white and black defendants would allow for a more exhaustive examination of the defendant attribution process. The development of more valid measures of victim evaluations, defendant evaluations, and defendant attributions would also improve the overall test of the model. A more reliable measure of defendant empathy would help to validate the finding that empathy toward the defendant has a small influence on sentencing in relation to empathy toward the victim. In addition, the relationship between pre-deliberation sentence positions and sentence outcomes should be tested with a sample with sufficient numbers to test for the moderating effects of race and evidence ambiguity. Finally, an examination of the *post hoc* empathy-based model with the inclusion of victim impact statements may shed some more light into how this evidence affects sentencing decisions. Although the current study was hindered by the factors described above, it is important to note that this study was a first of its kind in that it empirically tested a model of decision-making using data from real capital jurors. In addition, a model was developed that has practical significance for the courtroom. Sentencing schemes that focus jurors' attention on extralegal factors, e.g., victim evaluations, may be more likely to result in race-based sentencing than those that set strict limits on the types of non-statutory evidence that can be presented during the sentencing phase of the trial.

APPENDIX A

Variables Collected from Closed Ended Questions in CJP Interview

Case Factor	CJP Source	Question
Confession	Section IIIA, Question 3	Formal confession to authorities by defendant?
Eyewitness	Section IIIA, Question 4	Did any witness other than the police or an accomplice testify that he or she actually saw the defendant commit the crime?
Defendant provoked	Section IIIA, Question 6	Was the defendant provoked by the victim or others?
Intentional	Section IIIA, Question 6	It was an unintentional or impulsive act
Multiple offenders	Section IIA, Question 4a	Number of persons responsible for the killing?
Number of victims	Section IIA, Question 4a	Number of persons killed?
Victim/Offender relationship	Section IIA, Question 5	Were the defendant and victim related in any of the following ways?
Age of victim	Section IIA, Question 4c	Age (# Yrs)
History of violence	Section IVB, Question 1a	Was this factor in this case?

Note: these questions from the CJP interview were used to supplement the juror case summaries located in Appendix B and Lexis-Nexis published opinions.

APPENDIX B

JUROR CASE DESCRIPTIONS FROM CJP DATA

Note: The CJP did not provide a case description for every juror. This may be the result of a backlog in data entry or may be attributed to missing data.

Case # 6 (*n* = 3 jurors)

Fact	Mentions
Two defendants	2
Took place in grocery store	2
Robbery	2
Both defendants had guns	1
Shot employee	2
Shot customer (survived)	1
Only one triggerman	1
Defendant was on drugs	2
Defendant was triggerman	1

Case # 15 (*n* = 2 jurors)

Fact	Mentions
Robbery	2
Two defendants	2
Took place in a store I	1
Two victims	1
Accomplice did killing	1

Case # 105 (n = 3 jurors)

Fact	Mentions
Attempted murder	1
Robbery	1
Defendant went to buy crack from victim	1
May not have known victims in killing #1	1
Victim 1 ran away	1
Defendant shoots victim 2 (dies)	3
Defendant then comes across victim 3 and 4 in broken down car	2
Defendant robs Victim 3 and 4	1
Lets victim 3 leave	2
Defendant shoots victim 4 (dies)	3
Two weeks pass by	1
Defendant then goes to a crack house	1
Defendant shoots victim 5 in shoulder (survives)	2
Victim 5 tried to escape	1
Attempted robbery of victim 5	1
Defendant robs victim 6 (drug dealer)	1
Defendant shoots victim 6 (dies)	2
Drug turf war	2
Cousin testified	1

Case #108 (n = 5 jurors)

Fact	Mentions
Acquaintance/ informal relationship	4
Defendant asked her (victim) if he could come over	1
Went to victim's apartment	4
Defendant wanted a sexual relationship	1
Victim resisted	1
Defendant hit her	1
Defendant tied her up	1
Defendant raped her	4
Defendant choked her with towel	4
Defendant confessed to crime during unrelated arrest	3
Defendant was aware of what he was doing	1
Defendant was arrested after bank robbery	2
Defendant had raped women in the past	2
No witnesses to murder	1

Case #115 (n = 3 jurors)

Fact	Mentions
Drug deal	2
Robbery	1
Burglary	1
Kidnapping	2
Theft	1
Conspiracy	2
13 counts	2
Three victims killed	3
Two of the victims were drug dealers	1
Key witnesses worked at the gas station where they met	2
Three defendants (tried separately)	1
Met at gas station	2
Shot execution style	1
Bodies found in trunk	1

Case #116 (n = 4 jurors)

Fact	Mentions
The 2 defendants tried separately	2
Three offenders	3
Victim was skating in Berkeley	3
Defendants followed her to apartment	3
Kidnapped victim	4
Took her to ATM machine	3
Robbed her	4
Took her to the bay	4
Raped her	4
Tortured her (bite marks on body)	1
Shot victim	3
Victim drowned	3
Stole her car	4
Body found at park in water	3
Defendant took victim's car to crack house	2
Abandoned car in Oakland	3
Defendant was arrested first	1
Victim was about 20 years old	2
Witnesses from crack house testified that defendant talked about crime	1

Case #122 (n = 3 jurors)

Fact	Mentions
Two victims (drug dealers)	3
Drugs involved	3
Rival gang	3
Killed both victims at same time	2
Defendant picked a fight with the one in the car (victim)	1
Shot Victim 1	3
Shot victim 2	3
Victim 1 shot 3 times	1
Victim 2 shot once	1

Case #126 (n = 5 jurors)

Fact	Mentions
Victim & defendants were inmates	5
Murder took place on exercise yard	4
A guard saw 2 inmates from the tower, making stabbing motions	4
Three inmates involved	2
Four inmates involved	2
Five inmates involved	1
Hacked victim with prison made knives	5
Stabbed 9 to 10 times in the chest	1
In view of other inmates	1
Over turf/gang related (drugs)	5
Victim had drugs in hair	1
Premeditated	3
Two other inmates confessed	1

Case #127 (n = 4 jurors)

Fact	Mentions
2 murders	4
2 accomplices in first murder: were minors	3
Survivalists	1
One accomplice was lover of defendant	3
Accomplice instigated first murder	1
Accomplice hit him with machete in the back of the head first	1
Don't think they initially planned to kill Victim 1	1
Voted to kill him	1
Accomplices were living in golden gate	1
Second murder was just defendant	2
Some hint of drugs	2
Defendant claimed to be anti drugs	2
Gay prostitution	1
Defendant was threatened by victim 1 (job)	2
The 3 of them saw Victim 1 and took him to their tent	2
They were drinking	1
Shot victim 1 with BB gun 18-21 times	2
Victim 1 was injected with lice poison	1
Defendant raped victim 1	1
Defendant slit victim 1's throat from ear to ear	1

Case #127 (Continued)

Fact	Mentions
Accomplice stabbed v1	1
Victim 1 stabbed 8 times: 4 in front and 4 in back	1
Hand cuffed Victim 1	1
Beat Victim 1	3
Tortured Victim 1	2
Didn't have sex with victim 1	1
Defendant blamed accomplice	1
Accomplice blamed defendant	1
Mutilated body	2
They weren't caught	1
Defendant's lover (accomplice) left in September	3
Defendant looked for lover(II	2
Victim 2 told defendant he would tell him where lover was for $	2
Victim 2 was an acquaintance of defendant	1
Victim 2 upset defendant	1
Def. Was some type of pimp	1
Crime 1 was 6 months prior to crime 2	2
cut Victim 2's throat	3
Picked victim 2 up at Polk street	3
Had sex with victim 2	3
Defendant killed victim 2	2
Sodomized another victim	1
Defendant went to Washington	2
Picked up hitchhiker	2
Confessed to police about murders	3
Confessed to San Fran police	3
Implicated accomplices	2
Accomplice testified against def	1

Case #128 (*n* = 2 jurors)

Fact	Mentions
Husband hired someone to kill his wife	2
Bitter divorce	2
Defendant was supposed to bury victim, but didn't	1
Police officer found body	1
2 accomplices (husband and guy he hired)	2
Defendant kidnapped wife	1
Took victim to the country	2
Stabbed her 6 times	2
Defendant not triggerman	1
Life in prison	1
Stripped stolen car	1

Case #204 (*n* = 2 jurors)

Fact	Mentions
Drug related	2
Shot victim in the back	1
Defendant bought drugs, and then returned to steal drugs and $.	1
Victim tried to run into the house	1
Defendant shot victim	1

Case #212 (n = 4 jurors)

Fact	Mentions
Defendant knew the girl	1
Defendant lived in same apartment complex	1
Defendant was out with friends drinking	2
Defendant had blood on his pants	2
Witness saw defendant jump fence and throw shoes	4
Defendant stabbed her 17 or 27 times	1
Stabbed 33 to 34 times (II	2
Stabbed in front and back	1
Defendant denied doing it	1
Victim had rollers pulled out with her hair still in it	1

Case #216 (n = 3 jurors)

Fact	Mentions
Defendant went to victim's house	1
Defendant raped her	2
Victim was a young girl	1
Victim was mentally handicapped	1
Defendant hung around the house	1
Defendant found her alone	1

Case #219 (*n* = 4 jurors)

Fact	Mentions
Premeditated	1
Two accomplices	2
Defendant & friends confronted victim	2
Drove victim to wooded area	3
A fight broke out	2
Defendant put rifle to victim's head and killed him	1
Defendant shot the victim	3
Fit of rage	1
Victim was taking advantage of defendant's hospitality	3
Planned to scare victim	1
Lured him into car with pistol at bus stop	2
Victim was drug addict	2
Defendant tracked him down	1

Case #221 (*n* = 4 jurors)

Fact	Mentions
Defendant confessed	3
Stabbed victim 52 times	2
Victim was defendant's ex-girlfriend	4
Victim was killed in her house	2
Defendant said money was involved	1
Was a crime of passion	1
Defendant and victim got into a fight	3
Defendant was on drugs	2

Case #225 (n = 4 jurors)

Fact	Mentions
There were 4 people in a car	1
Two police officers approached the car	3
Defendants had escaped from prison	3
Shot the police officer	2
There was a shoot out	3
Car was illegally parked	1
Accomplice shot the officer	2
Defendant shot at the second officer	2

Case #503 (n = 4 jurors)

Fact	Mentions
Defendant was fishing	1
An officer wrote him ticket for fishing license	4
Defendant shot the officer in the back	4
Witnesses knew defendant was fishing at the spot	1
Heard a gun shot	2
There was a witness on the scene	2
Defendant took officer's ticket book	2
Defendant confessed	2
Defendant was arrested at a house where the car was hidden	1
Arrested for speeding by police	2
Another man was also shot	3
Rifle	1

Case #504 (n = 4 jurors)

Fact	Mentions
Victim was popular young lady	1
It was a brutal crime	2
Victim was raped	3
Stranger	1
Severely stabbed all over body	2
Witnesses said they saw him in neighborhood	1
Defendant broke into her home	2
Was in prison for manslaughter	2
trial was 3 years after crime	1
27 stab wounds	1
100 stab wounds	1

Case #516 (n = 1 jurors)

Fact	Mentions
2 accomplices	1
Robbery	1
Entered pawn shop	1
Victim shot once	1
Defendant was the triggerman	1

Case #606 (n = 1 jurors)

Fact	Mentions
Defendant robbed a convenience store	1
2 victims	1
Handcuffed them together	1
Shot both several times in head	1
1 died	1
1 paralyzed	1

Case #702 (n = 3 jurors)

Fact	Mentions
Robbery (drugs and money)	3
Defendant waited outside club for victim	1
There was an accomplice with him	2
Defendant frisked victim	1
Defendant had a gun	1
Victim had a gun	3
Defendant pistol whipped victim	2
Broke victim's nose	1
Intention was to get money	1
Defendant shot the victim	2
Gun went off by accident	3
A fight broke out	1
2 or 3 accomplices (one in car)	1
Victim was outside dealing drugs	1
Defendant fled the scene	1

Case #813 (n = 1 jurors)

Fact	Mentions
Defendant lured girl to apartment	1
Called victim up to come over for drugs if she would have sex with him	1
Lured victim into bathroom	1
Victim was having oral sex with someone	1
Defendant came in and shot her	1
Accomplice	1

Case #816 (n = 1 jurors)

Fact	**Mentions**
2 defendants	1
Robbed store	1
Shot a security guard	1
Several witnesses	1

Case #901 (n = 4 jurors)

Fact	**Mentions**
An accomplice testified	1
2 accomplices	1
Were at a club	1
Victim was businessman	2
Victim had money	2
Defendant wanted money for drugs	3
They were arguing in parking lot at club	1
Took victim down dirt road and killed him	1
Defendant stole and pawned guns	2
Defendant stole victim's gun	1
Defendant shot victim in face at close range with his gun	1
Defendant shot victim brutally	1
Victim pled for life	1
shot him 4 more times in head	1
Defendant was intoxicated	1
Robbed victim	1
All 3 defendants were friends with victim	3
Bragged about what they did	1
Had robbed a store in the past	1

Case #911 (n = 4 jurors)

Fact	Mentions
Kidnapping	3
Rape	3
Burglary	1
Defendant stole victim's car	2
Auto accident	1
Wanted a car	2
Wife wouldn't give defendant her car	2
Had marital problems	4
Took victim's car	1
Gave 3 nightgowns in car to girlfriend	1
Cops chased defendant	2
Abducted victim at mini mart	1
Came back and was picked up by cops	1
Took victim to a residence	2
Victim mailing something for new job	1

Case #926 (n = 3 jurors)

Fact	Mentions
Defendant confessed	2
Victim and defendant were friends	3
Shot victim	1
Shot victim 7 times	1
First shot in back	1
Shot him in head	1
Shot in the woods	2
Shot in corn field	1
Buried victim	3
2 accomplices	1
Killed a farmer as well	3
Shot farmer in head	3
Set farmer's house on fire	3
Defendant was hired to kill victim	1
Victim was going to law enforcement	1
Woman testified about plan to kill victim	1

Case #929 (n = 4 jurors)

Fact	Mentions
Defendant had been drinking	2
Police were called	2
Defendant tried to climb out of window	4
Aimed rifle and shot at deputy	2
The rifle went off	2
The shot hit deputy	2
Defendant was trying to sneak out of house to avoid police	2
Not clear if intentional or accident	1
Defendant hid in the woods	1

Case #1114 (n = 4 jurors)

Fact	Mentions
2 victims	2
Victim were killed at Baskin and Robbins	2
Defendant robbed owner	1
Murdered in back room	2
Shot at close range	3
Crime did not look like robbery	1
Defendant stole one of victim's car	1
Defendant was chased by police	1
Someone was with defendant	1
Never proved that he pulled trigger	1
Defendant was smoking pot	1

Case #1203 (n = 5 jurors)

Fact	Mentions
Defendant lived with woman for 10 years	3
4 people in house (2 kids)	1
Mother had mental problems	1
Threw defendant out of house	4
Mother moved in with new boyfriend	5
Defendant came over to try to get his child out of house	3
Defendant came back and set small fire on side of house	1
Boyfriend put out the fire	3
The oldest daughter woke up to smoke	1
They ran out of the house	1
Left children upstairs	1
Defendant was supposed to have been at sister's house at time of fire	1
Gasoline was poured at front and back entrance	3
4 children killed	4
Made statement that if he couldn't have woman and kids, no one could	1
Charged with arson	1

Case #1402 (n = 4 jurors)

Fact	Mentions
The victim was the defendant's girlfriends' 14 year old sister	4
Victim stabbed 25 times	3
Defendant came to house to pick up clothes	2
Was upset because girlfriend broke up with him	1
Mother came down and found the defendant in basement	2
Little girl was murdered in the basement	2
Defendant ran from crime	2
No motive	3
Defendant was arrested at sister's house	1
Defendant saw to assailants leaving house when he arrived	1

Case #1410 (n = 3 jurors)

Fact	Mentions
1 accomplice	1
2 accomplices	2
Defendant and cousin tried to take victim's purse	2
Put her in trunk	3
Cousin hit her in head with shotgun when she tried to escape	3
Drove to defendant's house	1
Cousin ran her over several times	1
Ran over several times	3
dropped her in ditch	3
Spray painted car	3
Used victim's credit cards	1
Robbed her house	2
Turned in on tip	1
Turned in by one of the defendants	1

Case #1418 (n = 3 jurors)

Fact	Mentions
Argument	3
Sot at drug dealer	2
Dug dealer used victim as a shield	3
Defendant told friends he was going to get victim back	1
Defendant shot 9 year old	3
Shot 3 times	1

APPENDIX C

CODEBOOK FOR LEXIS-NEXIS AND CJP DATA

<u>Prior history of violent crime</u>
0-No
1-Yes
9- NA

<u>Crime spree</u>
0-No
1-Yes
9- NA

<u>Contemporaneous crime</u>
0-No
1-Yes
9- NA

<u>Burglary</u>
0-No
1-Yes
3-INAP
9- NA

<u>Attempted murder</u>
0-No
1-Yes
3-INAP
9- NA

<u>Robbery</u>
0-No
1-Yes
3-INAP
9- NA

<u>Sex crime</u>
0-No
1-Yes
3-INAP
9- NA

<u>Kidnapping</u>
0-No
1-Yes
3-INAP
9- NA

<u>Peace Officer</u>
0-No
1-Yes
9-NA

<u>Outcomc</u>
0-Life
1-Death

<u># of victims killed</u>
Enter number

<u># of victims injured</u>
Enter number

<u>Beaten</u>
0-No
1-Yes
9-NA

<u>Bloody death</u>
0-No
1-Yes
9-NA

<u>Multiple stabbing</u>
0-No
1-Yes
9-NA

<u>Multiple gunshot wounds</u>
0-No
1-Yes
9-NA

<u>Single stabbing/cutting</u>
0-No
1-Yes
9-NA

<u>Weapon</u>
0-Other
1-Gun
9-NA

<u>Relationship</u>
1-Stranger
2-Other
9- NA

<u>Scene of crime</u>
0-Other
1-Victims' home/ place of work
9-NA

<u>Victim resisted</u>
0-No
1-Yes
9-NA

Multiple offenders
0-No
1-Yes
9-NA

Defendant was triggerman
0-No
1-Yes
9-NA

Multiple triggermen/ triggerman contested
0-No
1-Yes
9-NA

Confession
0-No
1-Yes
9-NA

Cover up
0-No
1-Yes

Arrested at the scene/escaping
0-No
1-Yes
9-NA

Intoxicated
0-No
1-Yes
9-NA

Torture/mutilation (several shots, stabbing, beating, etc)
0-No
1-Yes
9-NA

Rape or sexual motive
0-No
1-Yes
9-NA

Accomplice testimony
0-No
1-Yes
3-INAP
9-NA

Eyewitness to crime
0-No
1-Yes
9-NA

Someone heard def confess
0-No
1-Yes
9-NA

Child/ Minor(below 18)
0-No
1-Yes
9-NA

Senior (above 65)
0-No
1-Yes
9-No

APPENDIX D

JUROR PERCENTAGE AGREEMENT TABLES

- There were no published opinions for 32 cases
- Published opinions were found for 101 cases
- The Capital Jury Project dataset was used to supplement Lexis published opinions for 59 cases. History of violence was the most frequently missing variable in the published opinion, and the spontaneity of the crime was the least frequently missing variable.

General Information Lexis Published Cases

Variable	# of Times Missing in Lexis-Nexis Opinion
Violent History	46
Accomplice Testimony	10
Eyewitness to Crime	10
Witness Heard Confession	10
Defendant Confessed	10
Relationship	4
Victim resisted	2
Intentional/Spontaneous	1

- A two-thirds agreement rule was employed for coding variables
- When the two-thirds criterion was not met, the data were coded as 'missing'
- Jurors who reported that they were 'not sure' about a fact, or when the data were coded as 'missing', were not included in the ratio
    - For example, case A encompassed 5 jurors, and the jurors' responses for Relationship were coded as follows: juror A, 'not sure'; Juror B, 'missing data'; Juror C, 'yes'; Juror D, 'yes'; and Juror E, 'no'.
        - This case meets the two-thirds agreement rule; 2 yes: 1 no.

Juror Agreement Scores: Lexis Cases

Row	Case #	Violent History	Accomplice Testimony	Relationship
1	11	5 of 5		
2	12	1 of 1; 1 NA		
3	13	2 of 3; 1 NS	2 of 3	
4	17	3 of 3		
5	4		1 of 1	
6	9	2 of 2		
7	421	2 of 3	3 of 3	
8	424	3 of 5	5 of 5	
9	514	2 of 2; 1 NS		3 of 3
10	520			
11	602	3 of 4		
12	608	4 of 4		
13	1413	2 of 3	2 of 2	
14	1414	1 of 1		
15	1419	2 of 2; 2 NA		
16	703	3 of 3; 1 NA		

NS: Not Sure
NA: Missing Data

Juror Agreement Scores: Lexis Cases (Cont.)

Row	Case #	Eyewitness	Witness Heard Confession	Defendant Confession
1	11			
2	12			
3	13			
4	17			
5	4			
6	9			
7	421	3 of 3		3 of 3
8	424	4 of 5	4 of 5	
9	514			
10	520	4 of 4		4 of 4
11	602			
12	608			3 of 3; 1 NS
13	1413			2 of 2
14	1414			
15	1419	3 of 4	2 of 4	
16	703			

NS: Not Sure
NA: Missing Data

Juror Agreement Scores: Lexis Cases (Cont.)

Row	Case #	Violent History	Accomplice Testimony	Eyewitness	Witness Heard Confession
17	715	2 of 4; 1 NS			
18	724	4 of 4			
19	804				
20	806	3 of 3; 2 NS	4 of 5		
21	810	2 of 3	3 of 3		2 of 3
22	821		3 of 4	4 of 4	
23	824				1 of 1
24	905	3 of 4			
25	906	3 of 3			
26	910			4 of 4	3 of 4
27	918			3 of 3	2 of 3
28	930			4 of 4	
29	931	3 of 4		4 of 4	3 of 4
30	1501		2 of 3		3 of 3
31	1102	4 of 4			2 of 3; 1 NS
32	1104				1 of 1
33	1116	3 of 3			
34	1121	3 of 3			
35	1127	2 of 2			
36	109	4 of 4			

NS: Not Sure

NA: Missing Data

Juror Agreement Scores: Lexis Cases (Cont.)

Row	Case #	Defendant Confession	Victim Resist	Intentional	Relationship
17	715				
18	724				
19	804	2 of 2			
20	806				
21	810	3 of 3	2 of 3	2 of 3	
22	821				
23	824				3 of 4
24	905				
25	906				
26	910				3 of 3
27	918				
28	930				
29	931				
30	1501				
31	1102				
32	1104				
33	1116				
34	1121				
35	1127				
36	109				

Juror Agreement Scores: Lexis Cases (Cont.)

Row	Case #	Violent History	Accomplice Testimony	Eyewitness
37	133	2 of 3		
38	208	2 of 4; 2 NS		
39	218	2 of 3; 1 NS; 1 NA		
40	303	1 of 1		
41	308	3 of 4		
42	310	3 of 4		4 of 4
43	312	1 of 2; 1 NS		
42	310	3 of 4		4 of 4
43	312	1 of 2; 1 NS		
44	318	2 of 2		
45	1			
46	708			
47	850	3 of 3		
48	508	1 of 1		
49	1211	2 of 2		
50	922		2 of 4; 1 NS	
51	527	2 of 3		

NS: Not Sure
NA: Missing Data

Juror Agreement Scores: Lexis Cases (Cont.)

Row	Case #	Defendant Confession	Victim Resist	Relationship
37	133			2 of 3
38	208			
39	218			
40	303			
41	308			
42	310	3 of 4	4 of 4	
43	312	2 of 2		
42	310	3 of 4	4 of 4	
43	312	2 of 2		
44	318	2 of 2		
45	1			
46	708	4 of 4		
47	850			
48	508			
49	1211			
50	922			
51	527			

Juror Agreement Scores: Lexis Cases (Cont.)

Row	Case #	Violent History
52	807	1 of 2
53	815	2 of 2
54	18	1 NS
55	501	2 of 4; 1 NA
56	132	1 of 3; 1 NS
57	405	3 of 4
58	1506	1 of 2; 1 NS
59	1601	1 of 1

NS: Not Sure
NA: Missing Data

Table 2: Juror Agreement: No Published Opinion Cases

Row	Case #	Violent History	Accomplice Testimony	Eyewitness
1	105	2 of 3		
2	127	5 of 5		
3	6	1 of 2; 1 NS; 1 NA	2 of 3; 1 NS	2 of 3; 1 NS
4	15	2 NA	1 of 2	2 of 2
5	19	2 NA	1 of 1; 1 NA	2 of 2
6	105		3 of 3	3 of 3
7	115	2 of 2	2 of 2	2 of 2
8	116	2 of 6; 2 NS	6 of 6	6 of 6
9	126	5 of 5	3 of 5; 1 NS	
10	212		4 of 4	
11	216	2 NS; 1 NA	3 of 3	
12	219	4 of 4	2 of 4	3 of 4
13	221	4 of 4	4 of 4	4 of 4
14	225	1 of 1	1 NS	1 NS
15	504	3 of 4	4 of 4	4 of 4
16	516	2 of 2	2 of 2	2 of 2

NS: Not Sure
NA: Missing Data

Table 2: Juror Agreement: No Published Opinion Cases (Cont.)

Row	**Case #**	**Witness Heard Confession**	**Defendant Confession**	**Relationship**
1	105			
2	127			
3	6	1 of 3; 1 NS	2 of 3; 1 NS	
4	15	1 of 2	2 of 2	
5	19	1 of 2	1 of 1; 1 NA	2 of 2
6	105	1 of 3; 1 NS	2 of 3; 1 NS	
7	115	2 of 2	2 of 2	
8	116		5 of 6; 1 NS	
9	126	5 of 5	4 of 5	
10	212	4 o 4		
11	216		2 of 3	2 of 3; 1 NS
12	219		3 of 4	4 of 4
13	221		3 of 4	
14	225		1 of 1	
15	504		4 of 4	3 of 4
16	516		2 of 2	1 of 2

NS: Not Sure
NA: Missing Data

Table 2: Juror Agreement: No Published Opinion Cases (Cont.)

Row	Case #	Violent History	Accomplice Testimony	Eyewitness
17	606	3 of 3	3 of 3	3 of 3
18	702	4 of 4	3 of 4	4 of 4
19	813		1 of 2; 1 NS	1 of 2
20	901		3 of 4; 1 NS	3 of 4
21	926	2 of 4; 1 NS	2 of 4; 1 NS	4 of 4
22	929	3 of 4; 1 NS	4 of 4	3 of 3; 1 NA
23	1203	5 of 5	5 of 5	
24	1402	2 of 4	4 of 4	
25	1410	1 of 3; 1 NS		3 of 3
26	204	3 of 4; 1 NS		4 of 4
27	516	2 of 2		2 of 2
28	911	4 of 4	3 of 4	4 of 4

NS: Not Sure
NA: Missing Data

Table 2: Juror Agreement: No Published Opinion Cases (Cont.)

Row	Case #	Witness Heard Confession	Defendant Confession	Relationship
17	606	2 of 3; 1 NS	2 of 3	4 of 4
18	702	3 of 4	4 of 4	
19	813	2 of 2	1 of 2; 1 NS	
20	901		3 of 4; 1 NS	
21	926			
22	929	1 of 4; 2 NS	2 of 4; 1 NS	
23	1203	4 of 5	5 of 5	
24	1402	4 of 4	3 of 4; 2 NS	
25	1410	3 of 3	3 of 3	
26	204	2 of 4; 1 NS	3 of 4	
27	516	2 of 2	1 of 2	2 of 2
28	911	4 of 4	3 of 4	

NS: Not Sure
NA: Missing Data

Table 2: Juror Agreement: No Published Opinion Cases (Cont.)

Row	Case #	Violent History	Accomplice Testimony	Eyewitness
29	1114	3 of 3	3 of 3	3 of 3
30	128	1 of 1	1 of 1	
31	108		4 of 4	
32	204		3 of 4	
33	503		4 of 4	
34	1418	3 of 4	4 of 4	2 of 4
35	816	1 of 1	1 of 1	1 of 1

Table 2: Juror Agreement: No Published Opinion Cases (Cont.)

Row	**Case #**	**Witness Heard Confession**	**Defendant Confession**
29	1114	3 of 3	3 of 3
30	128	1 of 1	1 of 1
31	108		
32	204		
33	503		
34	1418	2 of 3; 1 NS	2 of 3; 1 NS
35	816	1 of 1	one 9

NS: Not Sure
NA: Missing Data

REFERENCES

Baldus, D.C., Woodworth, G., & Pulaski, C.A. (1990). *Equal justice and the death penalty.* Boston: Northeastern University Press.

Baldus, D.C., Woodworth, G., Zuckerman, D., Weiner, N.A., & Broffitt, B. (1998). Racial discrimination and the death penalty in the post-Furman era: An empirical and legal overview, with recent findings from Philadelphia. *Cornell Law Review,* 83(6), 1638-1770.

Barnett, A. (1985). Some distribution patters for the Georgia death sentence. *University of California Davis Law Review,* 18(4), 1327-1374.

Batson, C. D. (1991). *The altruism question: Toward a social—psychological answer.* Hillsdale: Erlbaum.

Batson, C. D., Polycarpou, M. P., Harmon-Jones, E., Imhoff, H. J., Mitchener, E. C. & Bednar, L. L. (1997). Empathy and attitudes: Can feeling for a member of a stigmatized group improve feelings toward the group? *Journal of Personality and Social Psychology, 72*, 105-118.

Bodenhausen, G.V., & Wyer, R.S. (1985). Effects of stereotypes in decision-making & information- processing strategies. *Journal of Personality and Social Psychology,* 48, 267-282.

Bodenhausen, G.N., & Macrae, N.C. (1996). The self-regulation of intergroup perception: Mechanisms and consequences of stereotype suppression. In N.C. Macrae, C. Stangor, & M. Hewstone (Eds.), *Stereotypes and Stereotyping* (pp. 227-253). New York: Guilford Press.

Bohm, R. (1999). *Deathquest: An introduction to the theory and practice of* capital punishment in the United States. Cincinnati: Anderson Publishing.

Bowers, W. J., & Pirce, G. (1980). Arbitrariness and discrimination under Post-Furman capital statutes. *Crime and Delinquency,* 26(4), 563-635.

Bowers, W.J., Sandys, M., & Steiner, B.D. (1998). Foreclosed impartiality in capital sentencing: Jurors' predispositions, guilt-trial experience, and premature decision-making. *Cornell Law Review,* 83(6), 1476-1556.

Bowers, W.J., Steiner, B.D., & Sandys, M. (2001). Death sentencing in black and white: An empirical analysis of the role of jurors' race and jury racial composition. *University of Pennsylvania Journal of Constitutional Law,* 3(1), 171-274.

Brewer, M.B. (1996). When stereotypes lead to stereotyping: The Use of stereotypes in person perception. In N.C. Macrae, C. Stangor, & M. Hewstone (Eds.), *Stereotypes and Stereotyping* (pp. 254-275). New York: Guilford Press.

Brewer, M. B. (1979). Ingroup bias in the minimal intergroup situation: A cognitive motivational analysis. *Psychological Bulletin,* 86, 307-324.

Brewer, M. B., & Campbell, D. T. (1976). *Ethnocentrism and intergroup attitudes: East African evidence.* New York: Sage.

Chiricos, T., Welch, K., & Gertz, M. (2004). Racial typification of crime and support for punitive measures. *Criminology,* 42(2), 359-389.

Brewer, T. (2004). Race and jurors' receptivity to mitigation in capital cases: The effect of jurors', Defendants', and victims' race in combination. *Law and Human Behavior,* 28(5), 529-545.

Cochran, J.K., Boots, D.P., Heide, K.M. (2003). Attribution styles and attitudes toward capital punishment for juveniles, the mentally incompetent, and the mentally retarded. *Justice Quarterly,* 20(1), 65-93.

Costanzo, M. & Costanzo, S. (1992). Jury decision-making in the capital penalty phase-legal assumptions, empirical-findings and a research agenda. *Law and Human Behavior,* 16(2), 185-201.

Darley, J.M., & Gross, P.H. (1983). A hypothesis-confirming bias in labeling effects. *Journal of Personality and Social Psychology,* 44, 20-33.

Death Penalty Information Center, *History of the death penalty: Part I, introduction to the death penalty.* Retrieved June 5, 2002 from http://www.deathpenaltyinfo.org/history2.html#/IntroductionoftheDeathPenalty

Deitz, S.R., Blackwell, K.T., Daley, P.C., & Bentley, B.J. (1982). Measurement of empathy toward rape victims and rapists. *Journal of Personality and Social Psychology,* 43, 372-384.

Diamond, S. (1993). Instructing on death: Psychologists, juries, and judges. *American Psychologist,* 48, 423-434.

Eagly, A.H. & Chaiken S. (1993). *The Psychology of Attitudes. Orlando:* Harcourt Brace & Co.

Edwards, K., & Smith, E. E. (1996). A disconfirmation bias in the evaluation of arguments. *Journal of Personality and Social Psychology,* 71(1), 125-147.

Ericsson, K.A., & Simon, H.A. (1980). Verbal reports as data. *Psychological Review,* 87(3), 215-251.

Fischhoff, B. (1975). Hindsight ≠ foresight: The effect of outcome knowledge on judgment under uncertainty. *Journal of Experimental Psychology: Human Perception and Performance,* 1, 288-299.

Foglia, W. (2003). They know not what they do: Unguided and misguided discretion in Pennsylvania capital cases. *Justice Quarterly,* 20(1), 187-211.

Fowler, J.F., Jr. (1995). *Improving survey questions.* Thousand Oaks: Sage Publications.

Gaertner, S.L., & Dovidio, J.F. (1986). The aversive form of racism. In J.E. Dovidio & S.L. Gaertner (Eds.), *Prejudice discrimination and racism* (pp. 61-89). San Diego: Academic Press, Inc.

General Accounting Office (1990). *Death penalty sentencing: Research indicates pattern of racial disparities* (GAO Publication No. GGD-90-57). Washington, DC: Author.

Gordon, R.A. (1990). Attributions for blue-collar and white-collar crime: The effects of subjects and defendant race on simulated juror decisions. *Journal of Applied Social Psychology,* 20(12), 971-983

Greene, E. (1999), The many guises of victim impact evidence and effects on jurors' judgments. *Psychology, Crime, and Law,* 5, 331-348.

Greene, E., Koehring, H., & Quiat, M. (1998). Victim impact evidence in capital cases: does the victim's character matter? *Journal of Applied Social Psychology,* 28(2), 145-157.

Gross, S. R., & Mauro, R. (1984). Patterns of death: An analysis of racial disparities in capital sentencing and homicide victimization. *Stanford Law Review,* 37, 27-153.

Haegrich, T.M., & Bottoms, B.L. (2000). Empathy and jurors decisions in patricide trails involving child sexual assault allegations. *Law and Human Behavior,* 24(4), 421-448.

Hamilton, D.L. (1981). Illusory correlation as a basis for stereotyping. In D.L. Hamilton (Ed.), *Cognitive processes in stereotyping and intergroup behavior* (pp. 115-144). Hillsdale, N.J.: Erlbaum.

Hamilton, D.L. & Trolier, T.K. (1986). Stereotypes and Stereotyping. In J.E. Dovidio & S.L. Gaertner (Eds.), *Prejudice discrimination and racism* (pp. 127-163). San Diego: Academic Press, Inc.

Haney, C. (1991). The Fourteenth Amendment and symbolic legality: Let them eat due process. *Law and Human Behavior*, 15(2), 1991.

Haney, C., Sontag, L., & Costanzo, S. (1994). Deciding to take a life: Capital juries, sentencing instructions, and the jurisprudence of death. *Journal of Social Issues,* 50(2), 149-176.

Hans, V. (1988). Death by jury. In K.C. Haas & J.A. Inciardi (Eds.) *Challenging capital punishment: Legal and social science approaches* (pp. 149-175). Beverly Hills: Sage.

Hans, V.P., & Vidmar, N. (1986). *Judging the jury.* New York: Perseus Books.

Hastie, R. & Kumar, A.P. (1979). Person memory: Personality traits as organizing principles in memory for behaviors. *Journal of Personality and Social Psychology,* 37, 25-38.

Holtz, R., & Miller, N. (1985). Assumed similarity and opinion certainty. *Journal of Personality and Social Psychology,* 48, 890-898.

Johnson, J.D., Simmons, C.H., Jordan, A., MacLean, L., Taddei, J., Thomas, D., Dovidio, J.F., & Reed, W. (2002). Rodney King and O.J. revisited: The impact of race and defendant empathy induction on judicial decisions. *Journal of Applied Social Psychology,* 32(6), 1208-1223.

Johnson, K.A. (1987). Black and white in Boston. *Columbia Journal Review,* 26, 50-52.

Johnson, J.D., Adams, M.S., Hall, W., & Ashburn, L. (1997). Race, media and violence: Differential aspects of exposure to violent news stories. *Basic and Applied Social Psychology,* 19, 81-90.

Kalvin, H., & Zeisel, H. (1966). *The American jury.* Boston: Little, Brown and Company.

Kan, Y.W., & Phillips, S. (2003). Race and the death penalty: Including Asian Americans and exploring the desocialization of law. *Journal of Ethnicity in Criminal Policy,* 1(1), 63-92.

Kashy, D. A., & Kenny, D. A. (2000). The analysis of data from dyads and groups. In H. T. Judd, & Charles M. Judd (Eds.), *Handbook of research methods in social and personality psychology* (pp. 451-477). New York: Cambridge University Press.

Keil, T. J., & Vito, G.F (1995). Race and the death penalty in Kentucky murder trials: 1976-1991. *American Journal of Criminal Justice,* 20(1), 17-36.

Kenny , D.A., Mannetti, L., Pierro, A., Livi, S., & Kashy, D.A. (2002). The statistical analysis of data from small groups. *Journal of Personality and Social Psychology,* 83(1), 126-137.

Kleck, G. (1985). Life support for ailing hypotheses: Modes of summarizing evidence for racial discrimination in sentencing. *Law and Human Behavior,* 9, 271-285.

Kline, R.B. (1998). Principles and practices of structural equation modeling. New York: Guilford Press.

Latzer, B. (1998). *Death penalty cases: Leading U.S. Supreme Court cases on capital punishment.* Woburn: Butterworth-Heinemann.

Lee, E.S., Forthofer, R.N., & Lorimor, R.J. (1989). *Analyzing complex survey data.* New York: Sage.

Leonardelli, G.J, & Brewer, M.B. (2001). Minority and majority discrimination: When and why. *Journal of Social Psychology,* 37, 468-485.

Loehlin, J.C. (1992) *Latent variable models.* Hillsdale, NJ: Lawrence Erlbaum Publishers.

Luginbuhl, J., & Howe, J. (1995). Discretion in capital sentencing instructions: Guided or misguided? *Indiana Law Journal, 70,* 1161-1182.

Lynch, M. & Haney, C. (2000). Discrimination and instruction comprehension: Guided discretion, racial bias, and the death penalty. *Law and Human Behavior, 24(3),* 337-358.

Marques, J.M., Yzerbyt, V.Y., & Leyens, J.P. (1988). The 'black sheep' effect: Extremity of judgments towards ingroup members as a function of group identification. *European Journal of Social Psychology,* 18, 1-16.

Macrae, C.N., Hewstone, M., & Griffiths, R. (1993). Processing load and memory for stereotype-based information. *European Journal of Social Psychology,* 23, 77-87.

Matlin, M.W., (1994). *Cognition.* Orlando: Harcourt Brace Publishers.

Mazzella, R., & Feingold, A. (1994). The effects of physical attractiveness, race, SES, and gender of defendant and victims on judgments of mock jurors: A meta-analysis. *Journal of Applied Social Psychology*, 24, 1315-1344.

McAdams, J. (1998). Racial disparity and the death penalty. *Law and Contemporary Problem,* 61(4), 153-170.

Mullen, B., Brown, R., & Smith, C. (1992). Ingroup bias as a function of salience, relevance, and status: An integration. *European Journal of Social Psychology*. 22, 103-122.

Murphy, D.E. (2004). 'Divorce was an option,' Laci Peterson's Mother Cries, *New York Times,* A22.

Murphy, E.L. (1984). Application of the death penalty in Cook County. *Illinois Bar Journal,* 73(2), 90-95.

Myers, B., Greene, E. (2004) The Prejudicial Nature of Victim Impact Statements: Implications for Capital Sentencing Policy. *Psychology, Public Policy, and Law,* 10(4), 492-515.

Neter, J., Kutner, M.H., Nachtsheim, C.J., & Wasserman, W. (1996). *Applied linear structural models*. Boston: WCB/McGraw-Hill.

Nisbett, R.E., & Wilson, T.D. (1977). Telling more than we can know: Verbal reports on mental processes. *Psychological Review,* 84(3), 231-259.

Nunnaly, J. (1978). *Psychometric theory*. New York: McGraw-Hill.

Pettigrew, T.F. (1979). The ultimate attribution error: Extending Allport's cognitive analysis of prejudice. *Personality and Social Psychology Bulletin,* 5(4), 461-476.

Pettigrew, T.F., & Meertens, R.W. (1995). Subtle and blatant prejudice in Western Europe. *European Journal of Social Psychology,* 25(57), 57-75.

Rabbie, J. M., & Horwitz, M. (1969). Arousal of ingroup-out-group bias by a chance win or loss. *Journal of Personality and Social Psychology,* 13, 269-277.

Rector, N.A., & Bagby, R.M. (1997). Minority Juridic decision making, *British Journal of Social Psychology,* 36, 69-81.

Raudenbush, S.W., & Bryk, A. S. (2001). *Hierarchical Linear Models: Applications andData Analysis Methods*. Newbury Park, CA: Sage.

Ryen, A.H., & Kahn, A. (1975). Effects of intergroup orientation on group attitudes and proxemic behavior. *Journal of Personality and Social Psychology,* 31, 302-310.

Sachdev, L., & Bourhis, R.Y. (1991). Power and status differentials in minority and majority group relations. *European Journal of Social Psychology,* 21, 1-24.

Sanderson, C., Zanna, A.S., & Darley, J.M. (2000). Making the punishment fit the crime and the criminal: Attributions of dangerousness as a mediator of liability. *Journal of Applied Social Psychology,* 30(6), 1137-1159.

Sandys, M, & Dillehay, R.C. (1995). First-ballot votes, predeliberation dispositions, and final verdicts in jury trial. *Law and Human Behavior*. 19(2), 175-195.

Sommers, S.R., & Ellsworth, P.L. (2000). Race in the Courtroom: Perceptions of guilt and dispositional attributions. *Personality and Social Psychology Bulletin,* 26, 1367-1379.

Sorensen, J.R., & Wallace, D.H. (1995). Capital- punishment in Missouri: Examining the issue of racial disparity. *Behavioral Sciences and the Law*, 13(1), 61-80.

Sorensen, J., Wallace, D.H., & Pilgrim, R. L. (2001). Empirical studies on race and death penalty sentencing: A decade after the GAO report. *Criminal Law Bulletin,* 37(4), 395-405.

Stahlberg, D. & Maass, A. (1998). Hindsight bias: Impaired memory of biased reconstruction? In W. Stroebe & M. Hewstone (Eds.), *European review of social psychology* (vol. 8, pp. 106-132). New York: Wiley.

Stets, J.E., & Burke, P.J. (2000). Identity theory and social identity theory. *Social Psychology Quarterly*, 63(3), 224-237.

Stevens, J. (1996). *Applied multivariate statistics for the social sciences.* Mahwah, NJ: Lawrence Erlbaum Publishers.

Sulzer, J.L., & Burglass, R.K. (1968). Responsibility attribution, empathy, and punitiveness. *Journal of Personality,* 36, 272-282.

Sweeney, L.T., & Haney, C. (1992). The influence of race on sentencing: A meta-analytic review of experimental studies. *Behavioral Sciences and the Law,* 10, 179-195.

Taijfel, H., & Turner, J.C. (1986). The social identity theory of intergroup behavior. In S. Worchel & W.G. Austin (Eds.), *Psychology of intergroup behavior* (pp.7-24). Chicago: Nelson-Hall Press.

Turner, J.C. (1982). Towards a cognitive redefinition of the social group. In H. Taijfel (Ed), *Social identify and intergroup relations* (pp 15-40). Cambridge, UK: Cambridge University Press.

Vandiver, M. (1997, March). *Race in the jury room: A preliminary analysis of cases from the Capital Jury Project.* Paper presented at the meeting of the American Academy of Criminal Justice Sciences.

Weiner, R.L., Prichard, C.C., & Weston, M. (1995). Comprehensibility of approved jury instructions in capital murder cases. *Journal of Applied Psychology, 80(4),* 455-467.

Weitzer, R. (1996). Racial discrimination in the criminal justice system: Findings and problems in the literature. *Journal of Criminal Justice,*24(4), 309-322.

Wilder, D.A., & Shapiro, P.N. (1984). Role of out-group cues in determining social identity. *Journal of Personality and Social Psychology,* 2, 342-348.

Williams, J.D. (1999). Basic concepts in hierarchical linear modeling with applications for policy analysis. In G.J. Cizek (Ed.), *Handbook of education policy* (pp. 473-493). San Diego: Academic Press, Inc.

Williams, M.R., & Holcomb, J.E. (2004). The interactive effects of victim race and gender on death sentence disparity findings. *Homicide Studies,* 8(4), 350-376.

SUBJECT INDEX

Aggravating evidence, 5, 22-24, 29-30, 32-33, 61-62, 72, 113, 146-147, 149, 152
    definition of, 9-10
    development of, *See* deathworthiness scale
    non-statutory, 15-18, 153-154
    weighing of, 11-13
Aggravation scale, *See* deathworthiness scale
Archival research, 2, 4, 21-23, 25-26, 35, 41, 47, 59, 60, 86, 148, 151
    limitations of, 32, 35-37, 61
Attribution, *See* defendant attribution process
Aversive racism, 26, 35, 49-50, 72, 147, 150
Baldus, David, 22, 25, 32, 34-35,
    39, 47, 62, 149
Baldus Study, 19, 30-32
    Charging and Sentencing Study, 31-32
    Procedural Reform Study, 30-31
Barnett, Arnold, 26-27, *See also* deathworthiness scale
Black male presence effect, *See* jury composition
Black sheep effect, *See* in-group bias
Bodenhausen, Galen, 51-54, 55-57, 69, 148
Bowers, William, 2, 23, 41-45, 60, 68, 69, 80-81, 85, 86, 97, 150
Capital punishment, 7-19
    death eligible, 9-10, 16
    Eighth Amendment, 8-9
    Fourteenth Amendment, 8-9, 19, 153
    Furman v. Georgia, 8-9, 18-19
    Gregg v. Georgia, 10-11, 14
    guided discretion, 9-19
    history of, 7-11
    jury discretion, 2, 7-9, 11, 23, 26
    McCleskey v. Kemp, 19
    non-statutory evidence, 1 4-18, *See also* aggravating and mitigating evidence
    sentencing phase, 2-3, 9-10, 16, 33, 40, 48, 51-52, 55, 56, 63, 69, 80, 155
    special issues state, 13
    Supreme Court and, 2-3, 5, 7, 14-15, 17, 19, 32, 59, 86, 153
    symbolic legality, 1-2, 19
    victim impact evidence and, 17-18, *See also*

victim impact statements
weighing process, 11-13, 33-34, 113
Categorization law, *See* in-group bias
Cluster sampling, *See* sampling techniques
Contemporaneous felony, *See* deathworthiness scale
Culpability scale, *See* deathworthiness scale
Death Penalty, *See* capital punishment
Deathworthiness scale, 21-22, 25-26
aggravation scale, 28-29
a priori method, 25-26, 30-32
Baldus study, *See* Baldus, David
Barnett system, 26-27
contemporaneous felony, 23,28-29, 31-32
culpability scale, 21, 29
development of, 86-88
empirical method, 25, 30-31
factors in, 87-88
results, 121-123, 139-143
supplementary homicide reports, 23, 24, 27, 29
use of, 95, 96, 99, 110
Defendant attribution process, 3, 39, 42, 43, 56, 62, 69-72, 77, 107- 108, 128, 130, 146-147, 154-155
attribution, 43-44, 48-49, 51-52, 56, 62, 75, 77, 99-100, 102, 106-107
attribution hypothesis, 3, 44, 52-54, 55-56, 71-72, 100, 102, 106-107, 146
defendant evaluation, 4-5, 68-69, 135-139, 149, 151-153, 155
disconfirmation bias, 45, 53-56, 71, 72, 102, 106-107, 149
external attributions, 2-3, 72
future dangerousness, 42-43, 48, 99-102, 106-108, 125-128, 130-131, 146- 147, 149, 154
heuristic hypothesis, *See* Bodenhausen or Wyer
internal attributions, 2-3, 42- 43, 48-50, 53-54, 56, 69, 71-72, 99-100, 102, 105, 147, 154
jurors' evaluation of mitigating evidence, 72, 77, 127, 128-129, 130-134, 136-137, 139, 146, 147, 149, 150, 152- 154
measuring mitigating evidence evaluations, 102-110
proof of future dangerousness, 102
stereotype and, 2-3, 48-49, 51-57, 69, 71-72, 74, 100, 105, 148-149, 151

Defendant evaluation, *See* defendant attribution process
Disconfirmation bias, *See* defendant attribution process
Dovidio, Jack, 1, 26, 72
Dual process model, 62-72, 77, 89, 91, 97, 109, 130, 145- 146, 151, 154, *See also* defendant attribution process and victim evaluation process
Egalitarian values, *See* normative structure
Empathy, 4-5, 75, 118, 119, 120, 121, 124, 145, 146, 152, *See also* victim evaluation process
  defining, 89
  measuring, 89-91, 94, 135
  towards the defendant, 68, 135, 136, 151-152
  towards the victim, 60, 63, 67, 91, 94, 117, 122, 130, 133, 135, 136, 151, 152, 153, 155
Experimental research, 2, 4, 46, 47-48, 56, 62, 148, 149, 151
  limitations of, 56-57, 59-61
  mock jury resaerch, 47, 56
External attribution, *See* attribution
External validity, 35, 47, 56, 59, *See also* validity
Gaertner, Sam, 1, 26, 72
Guided discretion, *See* capital punishment
Haney, Craig, 2, 16, 50-51, 54, 56, 60, 62, 71, 149-150
Heuristic hypothesis, *See* Bodenhausen or Wyer
Hierarchical Linear Modeling (HLM), 80, 84-85, 91, 96, 119, 122
Hindsight bias, *See* internal validity
In-group, *See* in-group bias
In-group bias, *See* victim evaluation process
In-group identification, *See* in-group bias
Instruction comprehension, *See* normative structure
Instruction guidance, *See* normative structure
Internal attribution, *See* defendant attribution process
Internal validity, 35, *See also* validity
  hindsight bias, 40-41, 45-46, 96-98
  impression management, 45
  sample selection bias, 35-36
  sample size, 36
Intraclass correlations, *See* statistical conclusion validity
Jury composition, *See* normative structure
Jury deliberations, 2, 4, 40, 43-44, 52, 57, 63, 82, 96-

97, 105-106,108-109, 145, 147, 150
Liberation hypothesis, 26, *See also* normative structure ambiguous
evidence and, 21, 35, 50-51, 54, 71
support for, 27, 31- 33
Mitigating evidence, 4-5, 10, 23, 29-31, 32-35, 39, 45, 54, 62, 113, 145, 149, 152, *See also* capital punishment
experimental research and, 56, 61-62, 71
jurors' evaluations of, *See* defendant attribution process
measuring, *See* defendant attribution process
non-statutory, 14-15, 18
weighing of, 11-13, *See* capital punishment
Mock jury research, *See* experimental research
Non-weighing states, *See* capital punishment
Normative structure, 3, 26, 40, 51, 63, 72-74, 77,147, 150, *See also* aversive racism
ambiguous evidence and, 16, 21, 26, 35, 50-51, 54, 56, 71-72, 151
black male presence effect, 40, 43-44, 51, 74, 113, 147-148, 150
clarity of, 3, 48, 63, 72, 74, 147
egalitarian values and norms, 1, 3-4, 19, 26, 40, 43-44, 48-49, 50-51, 56, 63, 72, 74, 77, 147, 150
instruction comprehension, 3, 19, 50, -51, 55-56, 74, 77, 110, 139, 148, 150
instruction comprehension, measuring of, 112
instruction guidance, 3, 69, 74, 77, 110, 139, 148
instruction guidance, measuring of, 113
jury composition, 3, 39-40, 43-44, 74, 77, 113, 150
liberation hypothesis, 26, 74, 151-152
racial tension and, 40, 49-51, 65, 68, 74, 147, 150
white male dominance effect, 43-44, 113, 139, 148, 150
Norms, *See* egalitarian values
Out-group, *See* victim evaluation process
Path analysis, 109-110
results of, 130-135, 136-142
jury score, 109
Post-hoc model, 136-139, 151-154
Post-trial interview research, 40-41, 47, 61

Capital Jury Project, 4, 40-41, 44, 60, 62, 66, 79-80, 82-83, 84, 85, 86, 99
instrument and method, 79, 81, 85-86, 92, 98, 101, 102, 104-105, 112-113, 135-136, 154
juror recall, 86, 97
limitations of, 45-46, 96
Race-of-victim effect, 2, 4, 60-61, 151
archival research and, 21, 22, 23, 24, 26, 28, 31, 32, 36, 47, 59
experimental research and, 48, 62
Race-of-defendant effect, 4, 50, 62, 148, 151
archival research and, 21, 23, 24, 35, 47, 59
experimental research and, 48, 60
Racial tension, *See* normative structure
Salience, *See* social categorization
Sample selection bias, *See* internal validity
Sample size, *See* internal validity
Sampling quotas, *See* sampling techniques
Sampling techniques, 79-86, *See also* statistical conclusion validity
cluster sampling, 80-81
multiple juror method, 84-85
paired sample, 99
sampling quotas, 80-81
single juror method, 85
testing the overall model, 108-109
Schema, *See* stereotype
Social categorization, *See* in-group bias
Social comparison, *See* in-group bias
Social Identity Theory, *See* in-group bias
Statistical conclusion validity, 82-85, *See also* validity
independence assumption, 82-83, 85, 117
intraclass correlation, 83-84
multi-level variables, 83, 84-85, 97
Type I and II errors, 82-83, 85, 107, 114
Stereotype, *See* defendant attribution process
Supplemental homicide reports, *See* deathworthiness scale
Taijfel, Henri, 64, 65
Triangulation, 31, 86, 87,
Validity, *See* internal validity, external validity, statistical conclusion validity, and archival, experimental, and post-trial interview research, limitations of

Victim evaluation process, 18, 42, 63-69, 108, 131, 145, 146, 148, *See also* empathy
- black sheep effect, 68-69
- categorization law, 63-64
- In-group, 3, 5, 42, 64-65, 66, 67, 89, 91, 94, 149, 152, 153
- In-group bias, 63, 65, 66, 67, 68, 149, 152
- In-group identification, 62, 65, 66, 67, 68, 69, 91, 94, 152
- Out-group, prejudice toward, 66-67, 68, 149, 152
- salience, 63 64
- social categorization, 62, 63, 66, 67, 69, 94, 146
- social comparison process, 62, 64, 66, 67, 68-69, 89, 91
- Social Identity Theory, 63-64
- victim evaluations, 3, 5, 41, 42, 44, 62, 63, 65, 67, 68, 75, 83, 94-95, 96-97, 108, 120-125, 129, 130-131, 133-134, 139, 145, 146-147, 149, 152, 153, 154, 155
- victim evaluations, measurement of, 92-94

Victim impact statements, 16-18, 59-60, 61, 153-154, 155
- *Booth v. Maryland,* 17, 44
- *Payne v Tennessee* 17-19, 63, 154

Wyer, Robert, 51-54, 55-57, 69, 148

Weighing state, *See* capital punishment